STECK-VAUGHN

TOP LINE *Math*

Pre-Algebra

Harcourt Achieve

Rigby • Saxon • Steck-Vaughn

www.HarcourtAchieve.com

1.800.531.5015

Acknowledgments

Editorial Director	Ellen Northcutt
Supervising Editor	Pamela Sears
Senior Editor	Kathy Immel
Associate Design Director	Joyce Spicer
Design Team	Jim Cauthron
	Joan Cunningham
Photo Researcher	Stephanie Arsenault
Cover Art	©Janet Parke
Photography Credits	p. 6 ©Bob Krist/CORBIS
	p. 30 ©Warren Morgan/CORBIS
	Additional photography by PhotoSpin Royalty Free and Royalty-Free/CORBIS

ISBN 1-4190-0372-0

6 7 8 9 10 1413 11 10 09

Contents

UNIT 1
Algebraic Expressions and Equations   6

UNIT 2
Equations and Graphs   30

UNIT 3
Patterns and Functions   46

UNIT 4
Inequalities   62

To the Student

Building a solid foundation in math is your key to success in school and in the future. Working with the *Top Line Math* books will help you to develop the basic math skills that you use every day. As you build on math skills that you already know and learn new math skills, you will see how much math connects to real life.

When you read the Overview in this *Top Line Math* book, read the You Know and You Will Learn sections. As you focus on new math skills, consider how they connect to what you already know.

Pretest and Post Test

Take the Pretest at the beginning of this book. Your results on the Pretest will show you which math skills you already know and which ones you need to develop.

When you have finished working in this book, take the Post Test. Your results on the Post Test will show you how much you have learned.

Practice

Practice pages allow you to practice the skills you have learned in the lesson. You will solve both computation problems and word problems.

Unit Reviews

Unit Reviews let you see how well you have learned the skills and concepts presented in each unit.

Test–Taking Strategy

Every test-taking strategy shows you various tools you can use when taking tests.

Glossary

Each lesson has **key words** that are important to know. Turn to the glossary at the end of the book to learn the meaning of new words. Use the definitions and examples to strengthen your understanding of math terms.

Setting Goals

A goal is something you aim for, something you want to achieve. It is important to set goals throughout your life so you can plan realistic ways to get what you want.

Successful people in all fields set goals. Think about your own goals.

- Where do you see yourself after high school?
- What do you want to be doing 10 years from now?
- What steps do you need to take to get to your goals?

Goal setting is a step-by-step process. To start this process, you need to think about what you want and how you will get it. Setting a long-term goal is a way to plan for the future. A short-term goal is one of the steps you take to achieve your long-term goal.

What is your long-term goal for using this book about pre-algebra? You may want to improve your test scores, or you may want to become better at math so you can become a real estate agent.

Write your long-term goal for learning math.

_____

_____

Think about how you already use pre-algebra. Then, set some short-term goals for what you would like to learn in this book. These short-term goals will help you to reach your long-term goal.

I can use pre-algebra in my everyday life to

☐ know how long I can drive on a full tank of gas.

☐ figure out how old my pet is in human years.

☐ convert metric units to customary units.

☐ figure out space travel using light years.

My short-term goals for using this book are

_____

_____

Pretest

Take this Pretest before you begin this book. Do not worry if you cannot easily answer all the questions. The Pretest will help you determine which skills you are already strong in and which skills you need to practice.

Write an algebraic expression. Let *n* be the unknown number.

1. 7 less than a number

2. 3 more than 4 times a number

Solve for $x = 2$ and $y = 4$.

3. $3x + y =$

4. $\dfrac{y}{2}(4 + x) =$

Write an equation.

5. The sum of a number and 2.5 is 8.

6. Seven is 4 less than a number multiplied by 3.

Solve.

7. $3 + 4 \times 6 =$

8. $3(n + 2) = 42$

9. $y - 4 > 6$

10. $4x \leq 12$

11. A painter charges $175 per day plus a flat fee of $75 for materials. He works on a job for four days. How much does he charge?

12. Clark scored 20 points. James scored 3 less than twice Clark's score. How many points did James score?

13. When a number, *y*, is divided by 5 the quotient is less than 3. What is the number?

14. Edgar earns $14 an hour at the sporting goods store. How many hours must he work to earn at least $280?

Give the next three terms in each sequence.

15. 2.5, 7.5, 12.5, 17.5,

16. 0.008, 0.08, 0.8, 8,

For items 17 and 18 use the coordinate plane below.
Give the coordinates for each point.

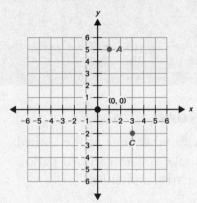

17. A _____

18. C _____

19. Use the table to find the function rule.
Then graph the function.

x	y
0	2
2	4
3	5

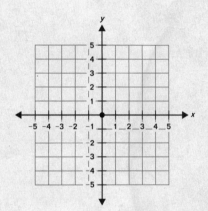

Find the slope.

20. $(2, 4)$ and $(3, 6)$ _____

For items 21 and 22 use the coordinate plane below.
Identify the *y*-intercept.

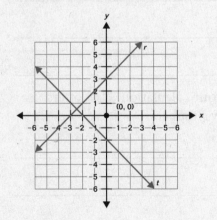

21. line *r* _____

22. line *t* _____

23. Make a table of values. Then graph the
equation $y = 3x - 2$.

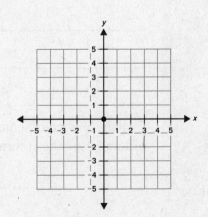

Algebraic Expressions and Equations

Real-Life Matters

You won a spot in a summer tour of the United States. The tour will take you to national parks, historic sites, theme parks, and cities.

People who plan trips use math to figure out costs and schedules. Knowing how to use algebraic expressions and equations helps them to plan quickly and accurately.

Real-Life Application

You are asked to help plan the tour. Your job is to buy *Teens Across America* T-shirts for everyone on the tour.

Suppose that you found T-shirts for $8 on the Internet. The sales tax is 5% and the shipping cost is $25 for the whole order. What is the total cost for 80 T-shirts?

_____

_____

_____

Write a sentence or equation that explains your calculation. Use letters (like *S* for shipping cost), but do *not* use any numbers.

_____

_____

_____

Explain how your sentence could be used to figure the cost for any item ordered over the Internet.

_____

_____

_____

Overview • Lessons 1-4

Writing and Solving Algebraic Expressions

The director of the *Teens Across America* program said, *This year, there will be just three fewer than twice the number of high school students who were on last summer's trip. Last year there were 39.*

Once you know how to use variables, you can easily figure out how many kids are going on the trip this summer. A **variable** is any quantity that can change or have different values. In math, you can use a letter to represent a variable or any unknown number.

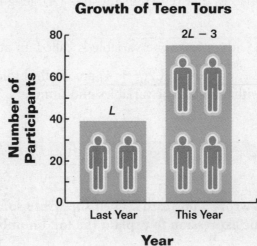

Growth of Teen Tours

YOU KNOW

- How to add, subtract, multiply, and divide integers

- How to simplify numerical expressions

YOU WILL LEARN

- To understand and write algebraic expressions

- How to apply the order of operations in algebraic expressions

- How to simplify and evaluate algebraic expressions

algebraic expression: $2n - 3$

variable

When you understand variables, you can write an **algebraic expression**, a math sentence that has numbers, operation symbols, and at least one variable. You will also be able to write an **equation**, a mathematical sentence that shows two expressions are equal.

Remember the BASICS

Solve.

1. $4 + (5 \times 2) =$

   $4 + 10 = 14$

2. $12 - (8 \div 2) =$

3. $(24 \div 6) + 2 =$

4. $(2 \times 5) + 15 =$

5. $(32 \div 4) \times 2 =$

6. $8 - 6 + (5 \times 3) =$

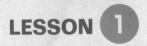

LESSON 1 Algebraic Expressions

When you do not know the value of a number, use a **variable,** a letter that stands for an unknown number. You already used variables in setting up proportion problems. You have also used variables to find the area of a rectangle ($A = l \times w$). In this formula, A, l, and w are variables that represent the area (A), length (l), and width (w) of the rectangle.

A mathematical expression with at least one variable is called an **algebraic expression.**

For example, $3n + 12$, $\frac{w}{5} - 7$, $m - n$, and $2(p + 4)$ are all algebraic expressions. Notice they have operation signs with variables or variables and numbers. They do not have an equals sign.

Example

Letisha wrote 3 postcards. Then she wrote some more postcards. Write an algebraic expression to explain the total number of postcards Letisha wrote.

STEP 1 Identify what you know and what you do not know.
Know: Letisha wrote 3 postcards.
Do not know: how many more postcards Letisha wrote.

STEP 2 Write a description of the situation in words.
Letisha wrote 3 postcards plus an unknown number of additional postcards.

STEP 3 Choose a variable for the unknown.
Let the letter a stand for the number of additional postcards.

STEP 4 Substitute numbers, operation signs, and variables for the words.

3   plus *unknown number* of additional postcards

3 $+$ a **expresses the total number of postcards Letisha wrote.**

ON YOUR OWN

The park where Diego works hired 12 fewer workers this year than it did last year. Write an algebraic expression for the number of workers the park hired this year.

Practice

Building Skills

Name the variable.

1. $6n + 5$

    The variable n stands for the unknown number.

2. $5w$

3. $m - 1.5$

4. $\dfrac{x}{8} + 3$

Write an algebraic expression.

5. 45 more than a number

    $n + 45$

6. n less than 20

7. the product of some number and 6

8. some number divided by 12

9. 3 less than 5 times a number

10. w less than y

Problem Solving

Write an algebraic expression.

11. The temperature dropped 5 degrees in the last hour. Write an algebraic expression for the new temperature.

     $t - 5$

12. Terrell's dog, Sparky, gained 8 lb in the last year. Write an algebraic expression that shows how much Sparky weighs now.

13. A clothing store sells gym shorts for $7.50 a pair plus tax. Write an algebraic expression for the total price.

14. Five friends equally shared the bill for lunch. Write an algebraic expression for the amount each friend paid.

15. At a chess play-off, your school's chess team received 2 points less this year than twice the number of points it received last year. Write an algebraic expression for the number of points your school's team received this year.

16. You earn $8 per hour. Your cousin earns more than you do. Write an algebraic expression that shows how much money your cousin earns for 6 hours of work.

LESSON ② Order of Operations

In math, addition (+), subtraction (−), multiplication (×), and division (÷) must be done in the correct order to get the right answer.

12 ÷ 6 is not the same as 6 ÷ 12. When you need to do more than one calculation you:

- Simplify within parentheses.
- Find the value of the number with the exponent. The exponent tells you how many times to multiply the base number.
- Multiply and divide from left to right.
- Add and subtract from left to right.

Example

Find the value of the following expression: $(4 + 6) \times 2^3 - 6$.

STEP 1 Simplify within the parentheses.

$(4 + 6) \times 2^3 - 6$
$(10) \times 2^3 - 6$

STEP 2 Find the value of the number with the exponent.

$10 \times 2^3 - 6$
$10 \times 8 - 6$ $\quad (2^3 = 2 \times 2 \times 2 = 8)$

STEP 3 Multiply and divide from left to right.

$(10 \times 8) - 6$
$80 - 6$

STEP 4 Add and subtract from left to right.

$80 - 6 = 74$

$(4 + 6) \times 2^3 - 6 = 74$

ON YOUR OWN

Find the value of $5 \times 3 + 8^2 - (12 - 3)$.

Practice

Building Skills

Find the value of each expression.

1. $60 - 3 \times 12$

   $60 - 3 \times 12 = 60 - 36 = 24$

2. $2 \times (3 + 5)$

3. $4 + 7 \times 4 - 3$

4. $3^2 + (4 \times 5)$

5. $30 - (10 - 7)^3$

6. $2 \times (3 + 5^2)$

7. $60 \div (12 + 3) + 5$

8. $(4^2 + 4)^2$

9. $5 + (15 - 6) \div 3 \times 5$

10. $36 \div (6 + 3)^2 \times 12$

Problem Solving

Solve.

11. Jack places his CDs on 7 shelves. He fills 3 shelves with 20 CDs and fills 4 shelves with 12 CDs. How many CDs does Jack own?

    $(3 \times 20) + (4 \times 12)$
    $60 + 48 = 108$

12. There are 6 schools in the city student council. Two schools each send 4 students to the council. Three schools each send 5 students. One school sends one student for every 150 of its 750 students. How many total delegates are there?

13. Alexis's book collection contains 23 mysteries, 8 novels, 3 science fictions, 9 biographies, and 2 histories. If she triples the size of her book collection, how many books does she have?

14. Milton does 80 push-ups, 120 sit-ups, and 30 pull-ups each day. Adrian only does half the number of sit-ups and push-ups that Milton does. But Adrian does 3 times as many pull-ups. How many push-ups, sit-ups, and pull-ups does Adrian do in one day?

15. Irma owns 20 audiobooks, or books on cassette. Cheryl owns 3 less than half that number. Irma offers Cheryl $5.50 for each audiobook in Cheryl's collection. How much money is Irma willing to pay for Cheryl's entire collection?

16. Add 11 to the sum of 3 squared and 5. This total is divided by 5. What is the final number?

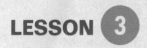

LESSON 3 Evaluating Algebraic Expressions

An algebraic expression contains at least one variable. Each variable stands for a number. When you know the numbers that each variable stands for, you can put the numbers in place of the variable and then use the order of operations to find the result. This is called *evaluating an algebraic expression*.

> **Algebraic Expressions**
>
> $\frac{p}{3} - 9$; $\quad 8x + 12y$; $\quad \frac{c^2 + \sqrt{d}}{e}$;
>
> $a + 8 - b + (-5)^3$

When you see a number in front of a variable, that means you should multiply the number times the variable. For example, $12y$ means that you multiply 12 times y, or $12 \times y$.

Example

Evaluate $10 + 5w$ when $w = 6$.

STEP 1 Put the number in for the variable.

$10 + 5w \quad \rightarrow \quad 10 + 5 \times \mathbf{6}$ ← $5w$ is the same as $5 \times w$.

STEP 2 Evaluate the expression.
Use the order of operations you learned in Lesson 2.

When you evaluate the expression, you do the calculations in the expression.

$10 + 5 \times 6 = 10 + (5 \times 6) = 10 + 30 = 40$ ← First multiply, then add.

When $w = 6$, $10 + 5w = 40$.

ON YOUR OWN

Evaluate $8t - 7$ when $t = 3$.

Practice

Building Skills

Evaluate each expression when $n = 4$.

1. $3n - 6$

$3n - 6$
$3 \times 4 - 6$
$12 - 6 = 6$

2. $n^3 \div (3 + 5)$

3. $4n + 7$

4. $24 - (4 \times n)$

5. $30 + (n + 7)^2$

6. $5n + (3 \times 2)$

Evaluate each expression when $n = -2$ and $m = 3$.

7. $m \times n$

8. $m \times (2 + n^2)$

9. $(m^2 + n)^2$

10. $5m + 5n - 5$

Problem Solving

Solve.

11. The number of dollars Selena has saved is expressed as $500 + 40m$, where m is the number of months since January 1, 2003. How many dollars has she saved when $m = 3$?

$500 + 40m = 500 + (40 \times 3)$
$\quad\quad\quad\quad = 500 + 120$
$\quad\quad\quad\quad = \$620$

12. The number of hours it takes to trim trees is expressed as $1 + \frac{15}{w}$, where w is the number of workers in the crew. How many hours does it take to do the job with 5 workers?

13. The number of miles Caitlin drove during a daylong trip is expressed as $60 \times 0.9h$, where h is the number of hours on the road. How many miles had Caitlin driven after 2 hours on the road?

14. The cost of wall-to-wall carpet is expressed as $18f + 6s$, where f is the square feet of carpet and s is the number of stairs. How much does it cost to carpet 250 square feet and 6 stairs?

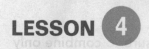

LESSON 4 Simplifying Algebraic Expressions

You know how to simplify fractions and ratios. Algebraic expressions can also be simplified. To simplify an algebraic expression, you need to know about **terms** and **like terms** and how to combine them.

Terms are numbers, variables, or numbers and variables combined by multiplication or division. These are examples of terms: n, $5n$, $\frac{n}{3}$, n^3, and -4.

Like terms are terms that contain the *same* variable with the *same* exponent. $3x^3$ and $5x^3$ are like terms, but $3x^2$ and $5y^2$ are *not* like terms.

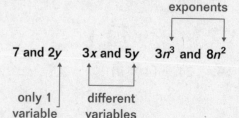

Simplify algebraic expressions by combining.

$$2a + 6b + 3a + b =$$
$$\underbrace{2a + 3a}_{5a} + \underbrace{6b + b}_{7b}$$

To simplify an expression means you write an expression that combines all like terms.

Example

Simplify. $3y^2 + 8x + y^3 - 2x$

STEP 1 Rearrange the terms so that like terms are next to each other.

$3y^2 \boxed{+\, 8x\; -\, 2x} + y^3$

$8x$ and $2x$ are like terms because the variable x is the same in each.
$3y^2$ and y^3 are *not* like terms because they do not have the same exponent.

STEP 2 Add or subtract to combine the like terms.

$3y^2 + 8x - 2x + y^3$
$3y^2 + (8x - 2x) + y^3$
$\mathbf{3y^2 + 6x + y^3}$

ON YOUR OWN

Simplify. $5n + 3np + 8np - 2n + p$.

Practice

Building Skills

Simplify.

1. $3y + 10x + 6y$ like terms

$(3y) + (6y) + 10x = 9y + 10x$

2. $4w + 7z - 2w$

3. $8n + 3n^2 - n$

4. $5 + 4xy + 3x - 2$

5. $4w + 8z - 5z + 6w$

6. $5w + 12w^2 - 3x - 8w$

7. $3(5 + 6n)$

8. $12(2y - 4)$

9. $6(9n + 5)$

10. $7(1 + t) + 4t$

11. $6(3p - 2) - p$

12. $10m + 3(m + n)$

13. $4(2t - 3) + 8$

14. $2 + 3(4x - 5)$

15. $2y + 3(4y - 2) + 6$

16. $4m + 3k - 6m + 2(k + m)$

Translating Word Phrases in Math Expressions

Learning how to translate words in math problems can help you select the operation needed to solve a problem.

You can use clues to help you decide which operation to use.

Operation	Clues
Addition	combine, and, increase, additional, total, sum of, more, altogether
Subtraction	difference between, less than, minus, how many more
Multiplication	times, multiplied by, product of, total
Division	divided by, divided by, divided into, separated into equal parts, divided between, shared equally between, per, for each

Example

Erin washes cars on weekends. She is paid $6 for each car she washes. Write an algebraic expression that describes the number of dollars Erin is paid for all the cars she washes.

STEP 1 Write an expression in words.
Six dollars times the number of cars

STEP 2 Choose a variable for any unknown values.
Let n equal the number of cars washed.

STEP 3 Write the algebraic expression.

six dollars	times	the number of cars
$6	×	n

Write the expression $6 \times n$ as $6n$.

TRY IT OUT

A cell-phone company charges $1.05 per minute when David uses a pre-paid phone card. Write an expression describing the price of a call for a certain number of minutes.

Circle the correct answer.

A. $1.05 ÷ m **B.** $1.05 \times m$ **C.** $m ÷ $1.05 **D.** $1.05 + m

Option B is correct. You can say *The cost is $1.05 times the number of minutes of a call.*

Overview • Lessons 5 – 9

Writing and Solving Equations

You have learned about variables and algebraic expressions. Now you will use these in complete mathematical sentences that show how different objects are related.

Suppose some apples and 2 lb of cheese cost $16. The apples alone cost $4. What is the price for 1 lb of cheese?

You can write an **equation,** a complete mathematical sentence that shows two expressions are equal, about what you know and do *not* know.

Start with a complete sentence.

Two times the cost of 1 lb of cheese plus $4 is $16.

Use the variable x for the price of 1 lb of cheese.

Two times *the cost of 1 lb of cheese* plus $4 is $16.

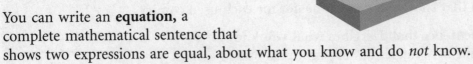

   2   × x +   4 = 16.

or

$2x + 4 = 16$

YOU KNOW

- How to use variables to write algebraic expressions

- How to simplify algebraic expressions

- How to use the correct order of operations

YOU WILL LEARN

- How to translate sentences into equations

- How to solve equations by adding, subtracting, multiplying, or dividing

---

Remember the BASICS

Write an algebraic expression for each.

1. 2 less than some number

   $n - 2$

2. 3 times a number

3. a number divided by 8

4. 3 more than twice a number

5. the difference between a number and 5

6. one-third of the sum of a number and 6

7. 4 times half of an unknown number

8. 62 plus a number

9. two-thirds of the product of a number minus 7

LESSON 5   Variables and Equations

An algebraic expression is a mathematical *phrase* containing at least one variable.

$3y + 7$ is an algebraic expression. Expressions do not have an equals sign.

An **equation** is an algebraic *sentence* that shows how 2 expressions are equal.

$3y + 7 = 10$ is an equation.

When writing equations use a letter that helps you remember what the variable means.

Example

At a comic book fair, Blake sold 4 brand-new comics and 6 used comics for a total of $170. He received $35 for each brand-new comic. Write an equation that shows how much he got for each used comic?

STEP 1 Write a sentence that describes what you know.
Four brand-new comics at $35 each; plus 6 used comics for some unknown amount; total = $170

> *Plus* means *and.*

STEP 2 Choose a letter to stand for the variable, or unknown quantity.
Let u stand for the selling price of a used comic.

> Use a letter that helps you remember what the variable means. The u here is for *used*.

STEP 3 Write an equation.

4 brand-new comics for $35 each	plus	6 used comics for some amount	equals	$170
4(35)	+	6u	=	170

The equation is $4(35) + 6u = 170$

ON YOUR OWN

The height of a picture frame is 8 in. The frame is 1.5 times as wide as it is high. Write an equation to find the width of the frame.

Practice

Building Skills

Write an equation.

1. A number subtracted from 12 is equal to 5.

   $12 - n = 5$

2. The sum of a number and 17 is 32.

3. The difference between a number and 3 is 8.

4. The product of a number and 5 is 30.

5. The quotient of a number divided by 8 is equal to 12.

6. When you multiply a number by 3 and then add 7, the total is 19.

7. Five times a number minus 12 is equal to 28.

8. A number added to 5.8 gives a total of 9.2.

9. Three less than the quotient of a number divided by 4 is equal to 6.

10. Forty-four is 4 more than the product of a number and 8.

Problem Solving

Write an equation.

11. The width of a cornfield plus 8 meters makes 73 meters.

    $x + 8 = 73$

12. The length of a rectangular swimming pool is 20 ft longer than the width of the pool, which is 15 ft.

13. Marco tutored a younger student for 45 min, which is 12 min less than Leanne tutored her student.

14. The movie ran 164 min, which was 14 min more than 10 times the length of the previews.

15. A state produced just 100 T of wheat over half what it produced last year. The amount last year was 150,000 T.

16. In 2 years, Kelly's age will be 75% of Laverne's age. Kelly is now 13.

LESSON 6 Solving Equations by Adding or Subtracting

If an equation contains a variable, you can solve the equation by finding the value of the variable that makes the equation true. That value is the **solution**.

For example, the solution to the equation $n + 6 = 10$ is 4. With n equal to 4, the equation becomes $4 + 6 = 10$, which is true. When you take the solution and plug it into the equation, the equation is true.

Example

Solve. $n + 14 = 19$

STEP 1 Subtract or add a number on both sides of the equation.
You add or subtract to get a zero on the side with the variable. To do this, you need to get rid of 14 by subtracting it on both sides of the equation

$$n + 14 - 14 = 19 - 14$$

STEP 2 Simplify.

$$n + 14 - 14 = 19 - 14$$

$$n + 0 = 19 - 14$$

$$n = 19 - 14$$

$$n = 5$$

STEP 3 Check your answer.
Replace the variable with the solution.

$$n + 14 = 19$$

$$5 + 14 = 19$$

$$19 = 19 \quad \text{The answer checks.}$$

Therefore, $n = 5$ is correct.

ON YOUR OWN

Solve. $y - 12 = 22$

Practice

Building Skills

Solve.

1. $x + 8 = 14$

   $x + 8 - 8 = 14 - 8$
   $x + 0 = 14 - 8$
   $x = 6$

2. $y - 5 = 3$

3. $n - 2.5 = 5$

4. $h - 16 = 7$

5. $w + 24 = 40$

6. $30 + n = 55$

7. $25 = 12 + y$

8. $w + 3.25 = 6.5$

9. $20 = m - 8$

Problem Solving

Write an equation. Then solve it.

10. Six students joined the photography club today. Now the club has 20 members. How many did it have before today?

    $x + 6 = 20$
    $x + 6 - 6 = 20 - 6$
    $x = 14$

11. The cooking club has 12 fewer members than last semester. This semester there are 15 members. How many members were there last semester?

12. The cleaning crew takes 5 hours to clean a movie theatre. That is 3 hours less than it takes to clean a concert hall. How many hours does it take to clean a concert hall?

13. Erika bicycled from her home to Loon Lake in 3.85 hours. This was 0.25 hours better than her previous fastest time. What was Erika's previous fastest time for bicycling to Loon Lake?

14. Amal bought a new camera for $85, which is $12.75 less than Hadiya paid. What did Hadiya pay?

15. Write your own addition or subtraction equation. Show all the steps in the solution to your equation.

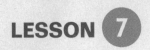

LESSON 7 Solving Equations by Multiplying or Dividing

You know that the key to solving an addition or subtraction equation is to get the variable by itself on one side of the equals sign.

Equations also involve multiplication, like $4n = 12$, or division like $\frac{y}{4} = 10$.

For a **multiplication equation** or **division equation,** you also want to get the variable by itself on one side of the equation.

Example

Solve. $\dfrac{n}{6} = 14$

STEP 1 Identify the number that is multiplying or dividing the variable.

$\dfrac{n}{6}$ is the same as $n \div 6$. Six is dividing the variable n.

STEP 2 Multiply or divide both sides of the equation by that number.

$\dfrac{n}{6} \boxed{\times 6} = 14 \boxed{\times 6}$ Multiply both sides by 6.

$\dfrac{n}{6^1} \times \dfrac{6^1}{1} = 14 \times 6$ The 6s cancel each other out.

$n = 14 \times 6$

STEP 3 Simplify.

$n = 14 \times 6 = 84$

$n = 84$

STEP 4 Check your answer.
Replace the variable with the solution.

$\dfrac{n}{6} = 14$

$\dfrac{84}{6} = 14$

$14 = 14$ The answer checks.

Therefore, $n = 84$ is correct.

ON YOUR OWN

Solve. $8m = 26$

Practice

Whatever you do to one side of the equation, you must do it to the other.

Building Skills

Solve.

1. $\dfrac{w}{7} = 14$

$w = 14 \times 7 = 98$
$w = 98$

2. $\dfrac{x}{12} = 4$

3. $8s = 88$

4. $12w = 60$

5. $\dfrac{t}{9} = 7$

6. $\dfrac{r}{4.5} = 6$

7. $32 = 0.5n$

8. $\dfrac{a}{8} = 5.4$

Problem Solving

Write an equation. Then solve it.

9. Gloria's mother is 2.5 times as old as Gloria. Gloria is 16. How old is her mother?

$x = 2.5(16)$
$x = 40$

10. Leon weighs 140 lb, which is 4 times what his dog weighs. How much does the dog weigh?

11. Anna spends one-fifth of her monthly paycheck on books. If she spends $50 per month, what is her monthly paycheck?

12. A low-fat turkey sandwich has 360 calories. This is 80% of the calories in a quarter-pound hamburger. How many calories are in a quarter-pound hamburger?

13. Decarlo ran 5.4 miles. This was 0.6 the distance Carrie ran. How far did Carrie run?

14. Kiersten bought 2 loaves of bread at $1.45 each. This represents $\frac{1}{8}$ of her grocery expenses for the week. What are Kiersten's weekly grocery expenses?

Solving Two-Step Equations

To solve an equation containing one operation, you performed the *opposite* operation on both sides of the equation. For example, you used subtraction to undo addition or division to undo multiplication. Your goal was to get the variable alone on one side of the equation. This same strategy works to solve equations involving two operations.

Subtraction to Undo Addition

$$t + 5 = 12$$
$$t + 5 - 5 = 12 - 5 \qquad +5 - 5 = 0$$
$$t = 7$$

Division to Undo Multiplication

$$8p = 24$$
$$\frac{8p}{8} = \frac{24}{8} \qquad \frac{8}{8} = 1$$
$$p = 3$$

Equations like $2n + 4 = 14$ involve addition *and* multiplication. You do 2 operations to get n by itself and solve the equation.

Example

Solve. $2n + 4 = 14$

STEP 1 Add or subtract from both sides of the equation.

$$2n + 4 - 4 = 14 - 4$$

$$2n + \quad 0 \quad = 14 - 4$$

$$2n = \quad 10$$

> First, undo addition or subtraction. Here you subtract 4 to undo the addition.

STEP 2 Multiply or divide both sides of the equation.

$$2n \div 2 = 10 \div 2$$

$$n = 5$$

> Next you undo multiplication or division. Here you divide by 2 to undo multiplication.

STEP 3 Check your answer.
Replace the variable with the solution, 5, for n.

$$2n + 4 = 14$$

$$(2x \times 5) + 4 = 14$$

$$14 = 14 \qquad \text{The answers checks.}$$

Therefore, $n = 5$ is correct.

ON YOUR OWN

Solve. $\frac{w}{6} - 3 = 6$

Practice

Building Skills

Solve.

1. $4p - 7 = 13$

$4p - 7 + 7 = 13 + 7$
$4p = 20$
$4p \div 4 = 20 \div 4$
$p = 5$

2. $2x + 1 = 17$

3. $\dfrac{n}{12} + 4 = 8$

4. $3w - 10 = 35$

5. $\dfrac{s}{6} - 3 = 2$

6. $12m + 2.5 = 38.5$

7. $\dfrac{y}{4} - 11 = 11$

8. $5x - 7 = 38$

9. $\dfrac{a}{4} - 7 = 10$

Problem Solving

Write an equation. Then solve it.

10. Nate's age is 3 years less than 2 times Ruth's age. Ruth is 8. How old is Nate?

$n = (2 \times 8) - 3$
$n = 16 - 3$
$n = 13$

11. When twice a number is increased by 12, the sum is 26. What is the number?

12. Ivan scored 4 points more than 3 times what Carl scored. If Ivan scored 28 points, how many points did Carl score?

13. Harry weighs 120 lb more than half of what his cat weighs. Harry weighs 130 lb. What does Harry's cat weigh?

14. Rita and Ian participate in a walk to raise money for charity. Rita walks 4 mi less than twice the distance Ian walks. Rita walks for 5 mi. How far does Ian walk?

Solving Multi-step Equations

Sometimes an equation can have more than 2 steps. You may need to simplify one side or both sides. Combine like terms or use the distributive property to make the problem easier to solve.

> For 2-step equations
>
> - First *undo* any addition or subtraction.
> - Then *undo* any multiplication or division.
> - Simplify.
> - Check your answer by substituting it for the variable in the original equation.

Example 1

Solve. $2n + 4 + 3n = 24$

STEP 1 Simplify the equation.
Combine like terms, if necessary.

Left side:

$$2n + 4 + 3n = 24$$

$$(2n + 3n) + 4 = 24$$

$$5n + 4 = 24$$

> **Like terms** are terms that contain the *same* variable with the *same* exponent.

> The like terms $2n$ and $3n$ are added to equal $5n$.

STEP 2 Add or subtract on both sides to undo addition or subtraction.

$$5n + 4 - 4 = 24 - 4$$

$$5n = 20$$

> You undo the $+ 4$ by subtracting 4.

> There is no more addition or subtraction to undo.

STEP 3 Multiply or divide on both sides to undo multiplication or division.

$$5n \div 5 = 20 \div 5$$

$$n = 4$$

> You undo $5n$ by dividing by 5.

> Solution.

STEP 4 Check your answer.
Replace the variable with the answer.

$$2n + 4 + 3n = 24$$

$$2(4) + 4 + 3(4) = 24$$

$$8 + 4 + 12 = 24$$

$$24 = 24 \quad \text{The answer checks.}$$

Therefore, $n = 4$ is correct.

ON YOUR OWN

Solve. $25(m - 2) = 650$

Practice

Building Skills

Solve.

1. $3w - 10 + 5w = 86$

$$8w - 10 = 86$$
$$8w - 10 + 10 = 86 + 10$$
$$8w = 96$$
$$w = 12$$

2. $\dfrac{y}{14} + 11 = 110$

3. $4x + 1 - x = 22$

4. $7a - a - 2 = 40$

5. $10x + 35 + 4x = 315$

6. $8n + 3n + 4 = 70$

7. $2(s - 1) = 16$

8. $12(m + 1.5) = 66$

9. $3(2n + 1) = 51$

Problem Solving

Write an equation. Then solve it.

10. All DVDs are on sale for $8 each during a special sale. You buy 6 comedies and a certain number of action movies. You spend $72, before tax. How many action movies did you buy?

$$8(6 + n) = 72$$
$$48 + 8n = 72$$
$$48 - 48 + 8n = 72 - 48$$
$$8n = 24$$
$$n = 3$$

11. If you multiply a number by 4, add 3 to that product, and then subtract 2 times the original number, the total is 15. What is the number?

12. Consecutive numbers are numbers in counting order. Two consecutive numbers have a sum of 17. What are the numbers? (*Hint:* Consecutive numbers are one apart. If you call the first of the numbers n, what will you name the second number?)

13. The price for using the batting cage is the same as it is for using the trampoline: $2 per minute. You reserve the batting cage for 20 min and the trampoline for a certain number of minutes. You spend a total of $64. For how many minutes did you reserve the trampoline?

TEST–TAKING STRATEGY

Use Mental Math

You can use mental math with algebra to answer test questions about equations.

Example

Nancy deleted 9 e-mails from her mailbox. She has 7 e-mails left. How many e-mails did Nancy start with?

STEP 1 Read the problem for cue words.
The word *deleted* is a cue word for subtraction. ·

STEP 2 Write an equation to model the problem.
Let *n* represent the number of e-mails Nancy started with.
What number minus 9 equals 7?

$$? - 9 = 7$$

STEP 3 Use mental math to solve.

$$16 - 9 = 7$$
$$n = 16$$

STEP 4 Undo the expression to check your answer.

$$9 + 7 = 16$$

So, Nancy started with 16 e-mails.

TRY IT OUT

A basketball team scored 42 points in the first half of a game. They ended the game with 89 points. How many points did the team score in the second half?

Circle the correct answer.

A. 47 points   **B.** 45 points   **C.** 131 points   **D.** 21 points

Option A is correct.
$42 + ? = 89$ Undo the addition: $89 - 42 = ? \rightarrow 89 - 42 = 47$.

Write an equation.

1. The sum of a number and 6 is 14.

2. The total is 48 when you subtract 12.

Write an algebraic expression.

3. three less than 8 times a number

4. four less than the quotient of a number and 5

Solve.

5. $2 \times 4 + 7$

6. $5^2 - (6 + 3)$

Evaluate for $x = 4$ and $y = 2$.

7. $3(x + y) - 5$

8. $(x^2 - 4y)^2$

Simplify.

9. $5n + (6 - 3n)$

10. $3(t + 5) + 4(r - 2)$

Solve.

11. $n - 8 = 10$

12. $x + 2.5 = 6$

13. $3x = 4.5$

14. $\dfrac{y}{20} = 0.5$

15. Julio took 22 min to finish the driving test. Carlos took 1.5 times as long. How many minutes did it take Carlos?

16. Hannah bowled a score of 90. Elena's score was 50 points less than double Hannah's. What was Elena's score?

17. When 3 times a number is decreased by 8, the answer is 52. What is the number?

18. The camping store sells items for $5 each. You buy 4 bags of trail mix and a number of meal packets. You spend $105 before tax. How many packets did you buy?

UNIT 2 Equations and Graphs

Real-Life Matters

How long would it take you to walk 3 miles? How about running that distance? Or covering that distance on in-line skates?

The table shows the type of traveling and how fast.

Type of Travel	Speed (in mph)
Walking	3
Running	6
Skating	12

Real-Life Application

Graphs are good tools for showing and comparing data.

This graph contains no numbers, but is based on the same data as the table.

How do the values for distance and time change as you move along one of the lines?

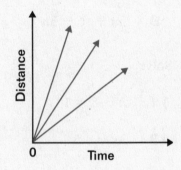

_____

How can you tell which line shows distance covered by skating?

_____

Which line shows distance covered by walking?

_____

If the runner stopped to rest for a while, what would the line look like for that period of time?

_____

Using the graph only, how could you tell which line shows the fastest speed?

_____

Overview • Lessons 10–12

Graphs

You have an out-of-town guest who has never been to your city. You want to identify the locations in your city for your guest to visit.

You sketch a map of the downtown area, which is a **grid** of streets. You label the borders of your map with letters and numbers.

Instead of trying to tell your guest to *go to the corner of Washington Street and Market Avenue,* you can simply say, *Go to 4B.* Your guest finds the vertical line labeled *4* and the horizontal line labeled *B.* Where the two lines meet is location *4B.* Your guest knows exactly where to go.

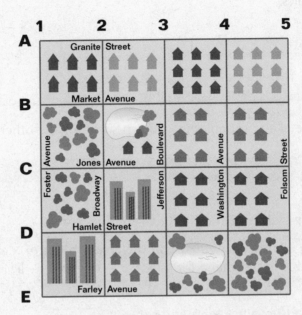

YOU KNOW

- How to solve an equation with variables on one side only

- That **integers** include all whole numbers, their opposites, and zero

YOU WILL LEARN

- How to solve equations with variables on both sides of the equals sign

- What a coordinate plane is

- How to graph equations on a coordinate plane

Remember the BASICS

Evaluate for $x = 2$ and $y = -3$. The first one has been done for you. If you need to review these skills, turn to page 18.

1. $4x + y$
   $4(2) + -3 = 8 + -3 = 5$

2. $2x - 3y$

3. $x - y$

4. $2x - 2y$

5. $x + 4y$

6. $3x + 3y - 4$

LESSON 10 Solving Equations With Two Variables

You have learned to solve equations that have one unknown number, or variable. Some equations have two variables.

$$y = 2x + 3$$

variable   variable

When you know what one of the variables is, you can solve for the other.

Example

Solve $y = 5x - 2$ for $x = 0$, $x = 1$, and $x = 4$.

STEP 1 Set up a table for plugging in the given values of x and finding y. The table is shorthand for *When $x = 0$, $y = -2$, when $x = 1$, $y = 3$, when $x = 4$, $y = 18$.*

STEP 2 Plug in the values for x and solve the equation for y. For each value of x (0, 1, and 4) you will plug that number into the equation. Your result is the value for y.

x	$5x - 2$	y
0	$5(0) - 2 = 0 - 2$	-2
1	$5(1) - 2 = 5 - 2$	3
4	$5(4) - 2 = 20 - 2$	18

STEP 3 State the value of y for each given value of x by using the form (x, y).

$$(x, y) = (0, -2), (1, 3), (4, 18)$$

ON YOUR OWN

Solve $y = 3x + 2$ for $x = 0$, $x = 2$, and $x = -1$.

x		y

Practice

Building Skills

Solve each equation for the given values of x.

1. $y = 3x + 2$ for $x = 0$ and $x = 2$

x	$3x + 2$	y
0	$3(0) + 2 = 0 + 2$	2
2	$3(2) + 2 = 6 + 2$	8

Solution: $(x, y) = (0, 2)$ and $(2, 8)$

2. $y = x + 4$ for $x = 1$ and $x = 2$

3. $y = 3x - 5$ for $x = 1$ and $x = 3$

4. $y = x - 7$ for $x = 1$ and $x = 4$

5. $y = 2x + 6$ for $x = -2$ and $x = 0$

6. $a = -b + 3$ for $b = 0$ and $b = 1$

7. $y = -2x - 4$ for $x = -2$ and $x = 0$

8. $y = 3x$ for $x = -2$ and $x = 2$

Problem Solving

Solve.

9. The number of square feet of lawn Mitch can mow is described with the equation $y = 700x - 50$, where y is the number of square feet of lawn and x is the mowing time in hours. How many square feet can Mitch mow in 1.5 hours?

$y = 700x - 50$
$y = 700(1.5) - 50; y = 1,000$

10. The money Jose earns each week is described by the equation $y = 0.12x + 200$, where y is the money he earns and x is the number of dollars of sales he is credited with. How much does Jose earn when he has $3,000 in sales?

11. Leila's expected test score can be described by the equation $s = 10h + 50$. S is the score and h is the number of hours she studies for the test. What score can she expect when she studies 3 hours for a test?

12. The distance Carmella drives when she is traveling 50 mph can be described with the equation $d = 50t$. D is the distance and t is the time in hours. How far does she drive in 4.5 hr?

LESSON 11 Graphing Points

When you cross a horizontal number line with a vertical one, you have a **coordinate plane.** The horizontal number line is the **x-axis.** The vertical number line is the **y-axis.** These axes meet at the **origin** (0, 0).

To name any **point** on the coordinate plane, think of the grid for your guest on page 31. You named the meeting point by using 2 points. You name any point on the coordinate plane the same way. You move right or left, up or down. You call each space on the plane a **unit.** For example, point A is 3 units (or spaces) to the right on the x-axis and 4 units (or spaces) up on the y-axis. The **coordinates** of point A are (3, 4). The coordinates are an **ordered pair** of numbers. You say *ordered pair* because the numbers have to be given in the correct order. The first number always tells you how far to move to the right or left from 0. The second number always tells you how far to move up or down.

To find the coordinates, count the way you do on a number line, using positive or negative integers. The x-coordinate is always followed by the y-coordinate, like in the alphabet, x then y.

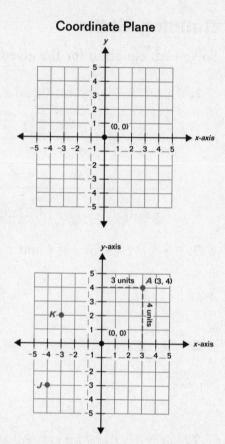

Coordinate Plane

Example

What are the coordinates of point K?

STEP 1 Find the x-coordinate.
Start at the origin (0, 0) and count to the left until you are directly below point **K,** to −3.

STEP 2 Find the y-coordinate.
Count up from −3 until you reach point K, to 2.

STEP 3 Name the coordinate pair for the point.

Point K is located at (−3, 2).

ON YOUR OWN

What are the coordinates of point J?

Practice

Building Skills

Using the coordinate plane below, identify the coordinates.

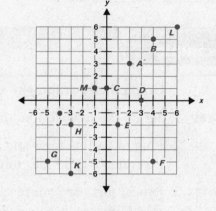

1. point F $F = (4, -5)$

2. point M

3. point A 4. point H 5. Point K

Name the point given by the ordered pairs.

6. $(4, 5)$ 7. $(3, 0)$ 8. $(-4, -1)$

9. $(1, -2)$ 10. $(-5, -5)$ 11. $(0, 1)$

Problem Solving

Using the coordinate plane shown above, name the points described on the coordinate plane.

12. the points with an x-coordinate of -4.
    Point J

13. each point whose x-coordinate and y-coordinate are identical

14. the points with a y-coordinate less than -2

15. the point 2 units up from and 2 units to the right of point A

16. the points that lie on an axis

17. the points with an x-coordinate greater than the y-coordinate

LESSON 12   Graphing Equations

The equation $y = x + 2$ is called a **linear equation.** If you graphed that equation on a coordinate plane, it would be a straight line. To make a graph of any linear equation, you can apply what you have learned about solving equations with 2 variables and plotting points on a coordinate plane.

Example

Graph the equation $y = x + 2$.

STEP 1 Set up the table to find ordered pairs.

STEP 2 Plug in a value for x and solve for y.
It is often a good idea to use 0 as your first value for x.

STEP 3 Repeat for 2 or 3 more values of x.
Select other values for x. Use both positive and negative integers.

x	y = x + 2.	y	Ordered Pair (x, y)
0	$y = 0 + 2$	2	(0, 2)
1	$y = 1 + 2$	3	(1, 3)
2	$y = 2 + 2$	4	(2, 4)
−1	$y = -1 + 2$	1	(−1, 1)

STEP 4 Plot the points on a coordinate grid.

STEP 5 Draw a line through the points.

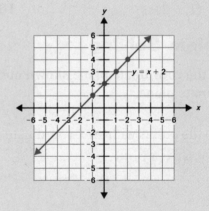

ON YOUR OWN

Graph the equation $y = 2x - 1$.

Practice

Building Skills

Complete each table. Then graph each equation.

1. $y = x + 3$

x	$y = x + 3$	y	Ordered Pair
0	$y = 0 + 3$	3	$(0, 3)$
1	$y = 1 + 3$	4	$(1, 4)$
2	$y = 2 + 3$	5	$(2, 5)$

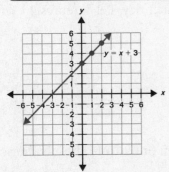

2. $y = x - 2$

x	$y = x - 2$	y	Ordered Pair

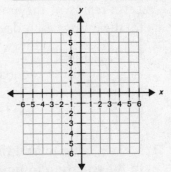

3. $y = 2x + 1$

x	$y = 2x + 1$	y	Ordered Pair

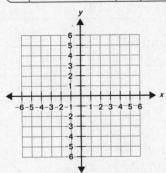

Problem Solving

Write an equation. Then graph the equation.

4. Ralph's brother Phil is 4 grades ahead of him in school.

Use the equation $y = x + 4$.

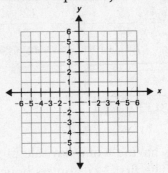

5. The temperature in Foster City is always 3 degrees lower than in Clarksville.

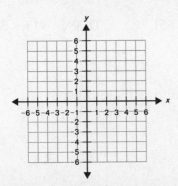

6. Whatever number Judy picks, Claire picks one that is 1 more than 3 times Judy's number.

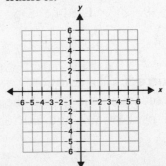

TEST-TAKING STRATEGY

Make a Table

You can make a table to help answer test questions about equations with 2 variables.

Jeff is paid $60 per day plus tips. On the first 4 days, Jeff got $4, $7, $10, and $12 in tips. What were Jeff's total earnings on each of those days?

STEP 1 Write an equation with 2 variables to model the problem.

Let x represent the amount Jeff was paid in tips each day. Let y represent Jeff's total earnings each day.

total earnings each day ($)	equals	salary per day ($)	plus	tips each day ($)
↓	↓	↓		↓
y	$=$	60	$+$	x

STEP 2 Make a table to find the solutions of the equation. Substitute the x-values in the equation to find the y-values.

Amount paid in tips each day ($) x	$60 + x$	Total earnings each day ($) y
4	$60 + 4$	64
7	$60 + 7$	67
10	$60 + 10$	70
12	$60 + 12$	72

Jeff's total earnings each day were $64, $67, $70, and $72.

TRY IT OUT

A sports shop is having a one-day sale in which customers can take $4 off the price of their purchase. The first 3 customers bought items that cost $12, $36, and $55. How much did each customer pay?

Circle the correct answer.

A. $16, $40, $59   B. $14, $34, $54   C. $9, $32, $51   D. $9, $13, $17

Option C is correct. The equation $y = x - 4$ represents the amount each customer pays. When you set up a table to find the solutions of the equation, you find that the first 3 customers paid $9, $32, and $51.

Overview • Lessons 13–14

Slope and *y*-Intercept

On a highway that goes down from a mountain area to a flat plain, you may see a sign like this one:

> **5% GRADE**
> Trucks test brakes and use lowest gear.

5% Grade

The sign means that the downward **slope** of the road surface is steep. Trucks with heavy loads have to be very careful.

You may have heard that slope is a description of how much a surface slants upward or downward. In math, slope is the steepness of a straight line.

The *y*-intercept of a line is the value of *y* where the line crosses the *y*-axis.

Remember the BASICS

Solve.

1. $4 - 5$

$4 - 5 = -1$

2. $-8 - 3$

3. $-4 - (-4)$

4. $14 \div (-7)$

5. $3 - (-5)$

6. $-24 \div (-6)$

LESSON 13 Slope of a Line

Slope measures the slant of a line from left to right. The **slope** of a line is a ratio. A ratio compares 2 numbers and is written as a fraction. Slope is a ratio of the vertical distance between two points on a line (the **rise**). Think about moving up or down. The rise is compared to the horizontal distance between the two points (the **run**). Think about moving left or right.

$$\text{Slope} = \frac{\text{rise}}{\text{run}} = \frac{(y_1 - y_2)}{(x_1 - x_2)}$$

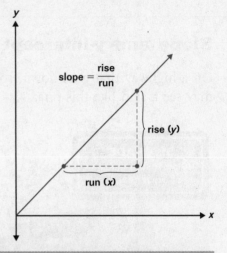

Example

What is the slope of a line that passes through points (6, 1) and (3, 4)?

STEP 1 Find the rise.
Subtract the y-coordinate of the second point from the y-coordinate of the first point

$(y_1 - y_2)$.

Write the **1** from (**6**, **1**) and subtract the **4** in (3, **4**)

$(y_1 - y_2) = 1 - 4 = -3$ The rise is -3.

STEP 2 Find the run.
Subtract the x-coordinate of the second point from the x-coordinate of the first point

$(x_1 - x_2)$.

Write the **6** from (**6**, 1) and subtract the **3** in (**3**, 4)

$(x_1 - x_2) = 6 - 3 = 3$ The run is 3.

STEP 3 Divide rise by run.

The slope is -1.

$$\text{Slope} = \frac{\text{rise}}{\text{run}} = \frac{-3}{3} = -1$$

ON YOUR OWN

Find the slope of this line.

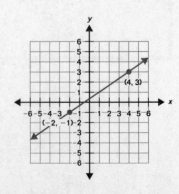

Practice

Building Skills

Find the slope.

1. $(-2, 3)$ and $(4, -1)$

$$\frac{(y_1 - y_2)}{(x_1 - x_2)} = \frac{3 - (-1)}{-2 - 4}$$

$$-\frac{4}{6} = -\frac{2}{3}$$

2. $(1, 2)$ and $(3, 10)$

3. $(1, 6)$ and $(4, 9)$

4. $(-3, -4)$ and $(1, 2)$

5. $(0, -3)$ and $(2, 7)$

6. $(-1, 4)$ and $(5, 4)$

7. $(-1, -3)$ and $(3, 7)$

8. $(4, -3)$ and $(4, 5)$

9. $(1, -6)$ and $(-7, -2)$

Problem Solving

Find each slope.

10.

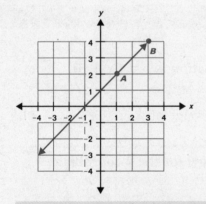

$$\frac{(y_1 - y_2)}{(x_1 - x_2)} = \frac{2 - 4}{1 - 3} = \frac{-2}{-2} = 1$$

11.

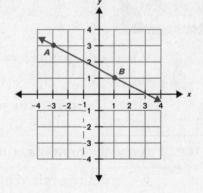

12.

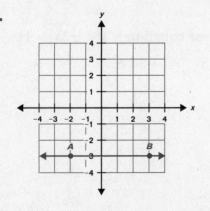

13.

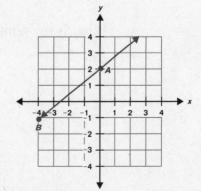

Using the y-Intercept

Slope is one important way to describe a line. The *y*-intercept of a line is another way to describe it. The **y-intercept** of a line is the point at which that line crosses (or *intercepts*) the *y*-axis.

The *y*-intercept of line *a* is 2. Its coordinates are (0, 2)

The *y*-intercept of line *b* is –3. Its coordinates are (0, –3)

You can find the *y*-intercept directly from the equation for a line. Let $x = 0$ and then solve for the *y*-intercept.

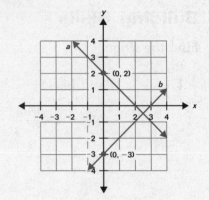

You can also find the point at which the line crosses the *y*-axis. Then read the coordinates at that point. On this coordinate plane the line crosses the *y*-axis at -1. The coordinates are 0, -1.

The *y*-intercept of line *c* is -1. Its coordinates are (0, -1)

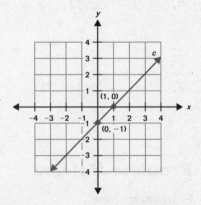

Example

What is the *y*-intercept of the line whose equation is $y = 5x + 3$?

STEP 1 Find *y* when $x = 0$.
Plug 0 into the equation for *x* to solve for the value of *y*.
$y = 5x + 3 = y = 5(0) + 3 = 3$

STEP 2 Name the coordinates of the *y*-intercept using 0 for the *x*-coordinate.

$y = 3$, so the *y*-intercept is at (0, 3)

ON YOUR OWN

What is the *y*-intercept of the line whose equation is $y = -2x - 4$?

Practice

Building Skills

Identify the *y*-intercepts for each line.

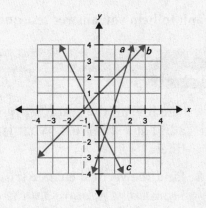

1. line *a*   (0, 3)

> Line *a* crosses the *y*-axis at $y = -3$.
> The coordinates of the *y*-intercept for
> line *a* are $(0, -3)$.

2. line *b*

3. line *c*

Find the *y*-intercept.

4. $y = 6x - 2$ **5.** $y = 3x - 1$ **6.** $y = x + 3$

> $y = 6x - 2 = 6(0) - 2 = -2$
> The *y*-intercept is at $(0, -2)$

7. $y = 7x + 4$ **8.** $y = -2x - 2$ **9.** $y = -5x + 1$

Problem Solving

Find each slope.

10. A line has a *y*-intercept of -3 and passes through $(2, 4)$. What is the slope of the line?

> $\text{Slope} = \dfrac{(y_1 - y_2)}{(x_1 - x_2)}$
>
> $\quad = \dfrac{-3 - 4}{0 - 2} = \dfrac{-7}{-2} = 3\dfrac{1}{2}$

11. A line travels exactly along the *x*-axis. What are the coordinates of its *y*-intercept?

12. There are two parallel lines. Line *d* has a *y*-intercept of -1 and line *e* has a *y*-intercept of -3. Which line passes closest to the origin?

13. Line *f* passes through $(3, 1)$ and $(3, 4)$? What is its *y*-intercept?

Use a Graph

You can use a graph to help you answer test questions about the slope of a line.

The line on the graph represents the slope of a hill at a ski resort. What is the slope of the line?

STEP 1 Find the vertical change (rise).
From point *A*, move 3 units up.

STEP 2 Find the horizontal change (run).
Move 4 units to the right.

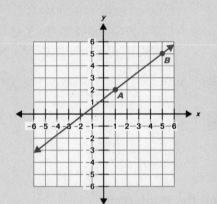

STEP 3 Write the slope as a ratio of vertical change to horizontal change.

$$\text{slope} = \frac{\text{vertical change}}{\text{horizontal change}} = \frac{\text{rise}}{\text{run}} = \frac{3}{4}$$

The slope of the line is $\frac{3}{4}$.

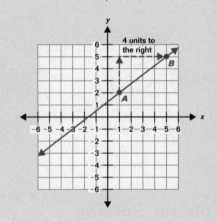

If point *B* on the graph above was located at (4, 4), what would the slope of the line be?

Circle the correct answer.

A. $\frac{1}{2}$ B. $\frac{2}{4}$ C. $\frac{2}{3}$ D. $\frac{4}{4}$

Option C is correct.

$$\text{slope} = \frac{\text{vertical change}}{\text{horizontal change}} = \frac{\text{rise}}{\text{run}} = \frac{2}{3}$$

Solve for y.

1. $y = 3x - 7$ for $x = 4$

2. $y = -x - 4$ for $x = -6$

Give the coordinates.

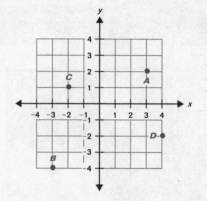

3. A _____

4. B _____

5. C _____

6. D _____

Graph each equation.

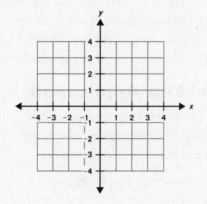

7. $y = x - 4$

8. $y = 2x + 3$

Find the slope.

9. $(2, 4)$ and $(3, 7)$

10. $(-2, 3)$ and $(0, 8)$

11. $(3, 3)$ and $(3, -2)$

12. $(0, 0)$ and $(2, 4)$

Identify the y-intercept.

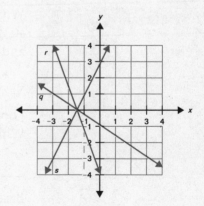

13. line q _____

14. line r _____

15. line s _____

Draw the graph of each line.

16. passes through $(2, -3)$, y-intercept $= -2$

17. passes through $(3, 0)$, y-intercept $= 1$

Patterns and Functions

Real-Life Matters

When you notice changes, see certain trends, or make guesses, you are relying on patterns.

You may think that there are more computers in schools now than there were few years ago. By looking at the graph, you can see how many students must share a computer and how this number changes as computers are added. Can you predict what the number of students to computers might be in the future?

Real-Life Application

The graph gives information that can be used to determine if the number of computers in schools is increasing.

What pattern does the graph show?

_____

Do you think the number of computers has been increasing in schools? Explain.

_____

What is the difference in the number of students who shared computers in 1983–84 and the number in 2001–02?

_____

Looking at the graph, which two school years showed the greatest change? Which showed the smallest change?

_____

Based on the pattern you see in the graph, can you predict the number of students per computer in 2002–03?

_____

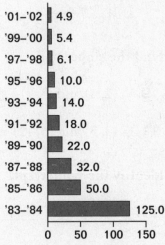

Students per Computer in U.S. Public Schools 1983–2002

School Year	Students per Computer
'01–'02	4.9
'99–'00	5.4
'97–'98	6.1
'95–'96	10.0
'93–'94	14.0
'91–'92	18.0
'89–'90	22.0
'87–'88	32.0
'85–'86	50.0
'83–'84	125.0

Overview • Lessons 15–16

Number Sequences

You have decided to join a CD club for a year. There are two plans you can choose. Both plans cost the same.

How many CDs will you have with Plan 1 or Plan 2 after 5 months?

No matter how you figure it, you will find that Plan 2 will get you many more CDs for the same price.

PLAN 1
Get 10 CDs the first month.
Get 5 CDs each month thereafter.

PLAN 2
Get 1 CD the first month.
Get 2 CDs the second month.
Get 4 CDs the third month.
Get 8 CDs the fourth month.
Get 16 CDs in the fifth month and each month thereafter.

You have already worked with **sequences,** or number patterns. You have used patterns to multiply or divide numbers by powers of 10. You also have used patterns and number lines to understand how to add and subtract integers.

In the next two lessons, you will use what you already know about numbers to make two kinds of organized lists called arithmetic and geometric sequences.

YOU KNOW

- How to write and solve algebraic expressions

- How to add, subtract, multiply, and divide integers and rational numbers

YOU WILL LEARN

- About arithmetic sequences

- How to find common differences and additional terms

- How to find common ratios and additional terms in geometric sequences

Remember the BASICS

Solve for each value of x. If you need to review these skills, turn to page 20.

1.

x	$x + 4$
0	4
1	5
2	6

2.

x	$3x$
0	
2	
4	

3.

x	$2x - 3$
0	
3	
6	

4.

x	$\dfrac{x}{2} + 3$
0	
2	
4	

5.

x	$-3x + 5$
2	
5	
10	

6.

x	$2x + 2$
2	
7	
12	

Arithmetic Sequences

Iris wants to keep a record of her exercises. On the first day that she began her exercises, Iris did 40 sit-ups. She plans to increase her sit-ups by a certain number of sit-ups each day.

Day	Number of Sit-ups
1	40
2	45
3	50
4	55
5	?

A **sequence** is a list of numbers that follows a pattern. Each number in a sequence is called a **term**.

The sequence 40, 45, 50, 55, ... is called an **arithmetic sequence**. Each term in an arithmetic sequence is found by *adding the same number* to the term before. Here are the terms in Iris's sequence:

40   45   50   55
$\llcorner$ +5 $\lrcorner$ +5 $\lrcorner$ +5 $\lrcorner$

You find each term in Iris's sequence by adding 5 (also called the **common difference**) to the previous term. The rule for this arithmetic sequence is *Add 5*. Add 5 to 55 to get the next term, 60. Add 5 to 60 to get the term after that. If it helps, think of an arithmetic sequence as another name for skip counting.

Example

What is the common difference in the arithmetic sequence 3, 7, 11, 15, ...?

What is the rule for the sequence, and what are the next 3 terms?

STEP 1 Subtract to find the common difference.
Start with the term or number at the end of the sequence and subtract the number that is before this term to find the common difference: $15 - 11 = 4$

STEP 2 Use the common difference to write the rule.
Keep subtracting terms to find the rule.

$11 - 7 = 4; 7 - 3 = 4$

The rule is *Add 4*.

STEP 3 Add the common difference to find the next terms. (For this example, add 3 times.)

$15 + 4 = 19; 19 + 4 = 23; 23 + 4 = 27$

The next three terms are 19, 23, 27.

Remember: The common difference in an arithmetic sequence may be a *negative* number.

ON YOUR OWN

Write the rule for the arithmetic sequence 4, 11, 18, 25, ...
Find the next 3 terms.

Practice

Building Skills

The first 4 terms of an arithmetic sequence are given. Find the common difference. Write the rule.

1. 18, 23, 28, 33, …

23 − 18 = 5, 28 − 23 = 5, or 33 − 28 = 5
The common difference is 5. The rule is *Add 5*.

2. 6, 13, 20, 27, …

3. 40, 36, 32, 28, …

4. 4.6, 5.8, 7, 8.2, …

The first 3 terms of an arithmetic sequence are given. Give the rule and the next 3 terms.

5. 12, 21, 30, …

6. 1.5, 4, 6.5, …

7. 200, 165, 130, …

8. 145, 134, 123, …

Problem Solving

Solve.

9. Alicia swims every day. She plans to swim three more laps each day than she swam the day before. She swam eight laps on Monday. How many laps will she swim on Thursday?

Start by finding the common difference, which is 3.

Mon.	Tues.	Wed.	Thurs.
8	11	14	17

10. Rajak increases the number of push-ups he does each day by 4. If he does 40 push-ups on day 6, how many will he do on day 11?

11. Each time Ulrika practices the piano, she increases the amount of time by 15 minutes. If she practiced Friday night for 50 minutes, how many minutes will she practice on Monday night?

12. Miguel does 20 sit-ups on day 1, 24 sit-ups on day 2, 28 sit-ups on day 3, and so on for 8 days. How many sit-ups does Miguel do in all during the 8 days?

LESSON 16   Geometric Sequences

There are 64 students competing in the state high school dance-offs. This table shows the number of dancers performing in each of the first 3 rounds of the dance-offs.

Round 1	Round 2	Round 3	Round 4	Round 5	Round 6
64	32	16	?	?	?

The sequence in the table shows another kind of sequence called a **geometric sequence.** Each term in a geometric sequence is found by *multiplying the previous term by the same number.* The number or factor that is used each time you multiply is called the **common ratio.** Here are the terms in this sequence:

64   32   16   ?

$\times 0.5$ $\times 0.5$

The rule for this geometric sequence is *Multiply by 0.5.* To find the next 3 terms in this sequence, multiply 16 by 0.5, then multiply that answer by 0.5, and multiply that answer by 0.5. The next 3 terms in the sequence are 8, 4, and 2.

Example

What is the common ratio in the geometric sequence 2, 6, 18, 54, . . .?

What is the rule for this sequence, and what are the next 3 terms?

STEP 1 Divide to find the common ratio. (Use 2 terms next to each other.)
Think: What do I multiply 2 by to get 6? *Divide* to find out: $6 \div 2 = $ **3.**

STEP 2 Use the common ratio to write the rule.
The common ratio is 3, so the rule is *Multiply by 3.*

STEP 3 Multiply the last term by the common ratio to find the next term. (In this example, do this 3 times.)
Start with the last term:

$54 \times 3 = 162$; $162 \times 3 = 486$; $486 \times 3 = 1{,}458.$

The next 3 terms are 162, 486, and 1,458.

ON YOUR OWN

Write the rule for the geometric sequence 2, 5, 12.5, 31.25, . . . Find the next 3 terms.

Practice

Building Skills

The first 4 terms of a geometric sequence are given. Find the common ratio. Write the rule.

1. 4, 10, 25, 62.5, . . .

> The common ratio is 2.5.
> The rule is *Multiply by 2.5.*

2. 3, 9, 27, 81, . . .

3. 1,024, 512, 256, 128, . . .

4. 0.2, 2, 20, 200, . . .

5. 30, 0.3, 0.03, 0.003, . . .

6. 788, 197, 49.25, 12.3125, . . .

The first 3 terms of a geometric sequence are given. Write the rule. Find the next 3 terms.

7. 2, 3, 4.5, . . .

8. 800, 400, 200, . . .

9. 0.4, 40, 4,000, . . .

10. 0.2, 0.04, 0.008, . . .

11. 0.25, 5, 100, . . .

12. 5, 25, 125, . . .

Problem Solving

Solve.

13. What is the next term in the geometric sequence 6, 300, 15,000, . . .?

> The rule is multiply by 50.
> The next term is $15,000 \times 50 = 750,000$.

14. What is the next term in the geometric sequence 2, 6, 18, . . .?

15. Ramón drank 2 glasses of milk on Monday. On Tuesday he drank half as much. On Wednesday, he drank half as much again. How many glasses of milk will he drink on Thursday? On Friday?

16. Here are Julia's scores for the science contest: 450, 45, and 4.5. Use this sequence to find her next 3 possible scores.

17. In a 16-team play-off, 8 teams will lose on the first day. How many teams will play on the second day? How many games will be played before there is a winner of the play-off?

18. Sixty-four bands entered a competition. If half of the bands lose after each round of the competition, how many rounds will there be before there is a winner?

TEST-TAKING STRATEGY

Find a Pattern

Finding a pattern can help you answer test questions about arithmetic sequences.

Example

Rita is in a 6-week training program for a marathon. The table shows her running schedule. If the pattern keeps going, how many miles will Rita run in the 6th week?

Week	1	2	3	4	5	6
Miles	10	13	16	19	22	?

STEP 1 Find a pattern.

Here, the pattern shows the number of miles Rita ran each week.

Week	1	2	3	4	5	6
Miles	10	13	16	19	22	?

+3 +3 +3 +3

Pattern: Start with 10 and add 3 over and over.

STEP 2 Use the pattern to find the next numbers.

Here, adding 3 shows the number of miles Rita will run in the 6th week.

$22 + 3 = 25$

If the pattern keeps going, Rita will run 25 miles in week 6.

TRY IT OUT

The price of a gallon of gasoline was $1.57 in April. In May, the price went up to $1.67. The price reached $1.77 in June and $1.87 in July. Find the pattern in the gasoline prices. If the pattern continues, what will the price of a gallon of gasoline be in August?

Circle the answer.

A. $2.07   B. $1.97   C. $1.87   D. $1.94

Option B is correct.

The pattern is a $0.10 increase in price for each month. August is the next month. The price in August would be $1.87 + $0.10 = $1.97.

Overview • Lessons 17–19

Functions

You have found 2 online music companies that let you download songs. Both companies charge a fee to listen to music. You can listen to as much music as you want to until your subscription ends.

Company **A**

$10 per month,
$1 per song kept

Company **B**

$12 per month,
$0.50 per song kept

Both companies charge a flat rate per song for any music that you keep and burn onto a CD.

Which company should you choose? Finding a pattern can help you answer the question. Now that you know about patterns and sequences, you will learn about **functions,** how to use tables to find patterns of numbers, and how to graph functions on the coordinate plane.

YOU KNOW

- How to find common differences and additional terms in arithmetic sequences

- How to find common ratios and additional terms in geometric sequences

- How to graph points on a coordinate plane

- How to solve and graph equations with two variables

YOU WILL LEARN

- How to use tables to find and continue number patterns

- Function rules

- How to use function tables and function rules to graph equations on the coordinate plane

Remember the BASICS

Solve for each given value of x. If you need to review these skills, turn to page 20

1.	x	$3x + 4$
	0	4
	1	7
	2	10

2.	x	$2x + 3$
	−1	
	0	
	1	

3.	x	$4(x - 2)$
	0	
	4	
	8	

4.	x	$-3x - 3$
	−2	
	0	
	2	

5.	x	$\dfrac{x}{4} + 4$
	−4	
	0	
	4	

6.	x	$6x$
	0	
	1	
	2	

LESSON 17 Patterns and Tables

Your service club is having a car wash. You charge $5 to wash one car. Your group washes about 8 cars every hour.

The table below shows how much money your club can expect to make. Study the table to find each rule.

Hours worked	1	2	3	4	5	6	7
Cars washed	8	16	24	?	?	?	?
Money earned at $5 rate	$40	$80	$120	?	?	?	?

For hours worked: Start with 1; add 1.
For cars washed: Start with 8; add 8.
For money earned: Start with $40; add $40.

Using a table like this can help you find out how much money you can expect to earn.

Example

How much money will you earn if you washed cars for 6 hours?

STEP 1 Find the pattern.
Read across the row for Money earned at $5 rate. Find the common difference between each pair of items.

Think: Subtract any 2 terms that are next to each other to find the common difference. The pattern is *Add $40.*

STEP 2 Add to continue the pattern.
(Stop when you reach the column for 6 hours worked.)

$120 **+** **$40** = $160; $160 **+** **$40** = $200; $200 **+** **$40** = $240.

You raise $240 by washing cars for 6 hours.

ON YOUR OWN

Use the table. How many cars will your group wash in 7 hours?

Practice

Building Skills

At a local movie rental store you can pay $15 per month and then rent up to five DVDs. If the store delivers to your house, they charge another fee for every DVD they deliver. The table below shows the number of DVDs and the cost for delivery. Use the information in the table to solve Problems 1–6.

DVDs delivered	1	2	3	4	5	6
Price in dollars	4	8	12	?	?	?

1. You pay $15 for 1 month but have only 4 movies delivered. What is your total cost?

> You pay $4 per video. Therefore, to rent 4 DVDs you would pay $12 + $16, or $28.

2. What is the delivery fee alone for 5 movies? For 7 movies?

3. How much do you pay for a one-month fee and 6 movie deliveries?

4. How much do you pay for 3 months and 2 movie deliveries each month?

5. How much do you pay for 6 months and 3 movie deliveries each month?

6. You pay for 6 months and have some movies delivered. The total price you pay is $150. How many movies were delivered during that time?

The tax table shows cashiers the total price of an item including sales tax of 6%. Use the information in the table to solve Problems 7–12.

Price (in dollars)	1	2	3	4	5	6
Amount of Tax at 6%	$0.06	$0.12	$0.18	?	?	?
Total Price	$1.06	$2.12	$3.18	?	?	?

7. What is the total price of a $4 item with sales tax of 6%?

> The pattern is $2.12 − $1.06 = $1.06
> Four items will be
> $3.18 + $1.06 = $4.24.

8. What is the amount of tax on a $5 item?

9. What is the total price of a $6 item?

10. What would the tax be on an $8 item? How much is the total price?

11. A person buys a $3 item and a $7 item. How much does the person pay in all?

12. A person pays $7.42 for an item, including tax. What is the price of the item before tax?

LESSON ⑱ Functions and Function Rules

Sarita has an after-school job. She is paid $12 per hour.

The amount of money Sarita earns is a *function* of the number of hours she works.

A **function** pairs 2 sets of numbers. That means that for each number in the first set, there is exactly 1 number in the second set.

> Remember: If you have ever used an input-output machine to do math, you have used a function table.

A **function table** has input values and output values. For any input value in a function table, there is only one output value. The table below shows the rate at which Sarita earns money at her job.

Input: Number of hours worked	1	8	16	24	32	40
Output: Total dollars earned	12	96	192	288	384	480

The dollars that Sarita earns (output) is a function of the number of hours she works (input) multiplied by her hourly pay rate. Since she earns $12 per hour, the table shows that every output value is 12 times every input value.

A **function rule** is an equation that shows the relationship between inputs and outputs. Here is a function rule for finding Sarita's total pay: $T = hd$,

T = total dollars earned, h = hours worked, and d = dollars paid per hour.

Example

How much money will Sarita earn if she works 30 hours?

Think: The total number of dollars she earns is a function of the number of hours she works multiplied by 12.

STEP 1 Write a function rule.
For Sarita's total pay, the rule is $T = hd$.

STEP 2 Substitute values and solve.
In this example, substitute numbers for h and d.

$T = hd \rightarrow T = 30(12) = 360$

Sarita earns $360 for 30 hours of work.

ON YOUR OWN

Eric also has an after-school job. The function table shows Eric's pay for hours worked. If Eric works 24 hours, what would his total pay be?

Hours worked	1	4	8	12	16	20
Total pay in dollars	9	36	72	108	144	180

Practice

Building Skills

Complete each function table. Then write a function rule for each.

1.

Input x	1	2	3	4	5	6
Output y	5	10	15	20	25	30

The function rule for the relationship between the input values and output values is $y = 5x$.

2.

Input a	2	4	6	?	?	12
Output b	6	12	?	24	30	?

Is the table a function table? Write *Yes* or *No*. Explain your answer. Remember that for each input value in a function table, there is only one output value.

3.

Input	1	2	3	4	5	6
Output	5	6	7	8	10	12

4.

Input	2	6	18	54	24	12
Output	3	9	27	81	36	18

Problem Solving

Solve.

5. Ted's pay is a function of the number of hours he works multiplied by his hourly wage. How much will he earn in 24 hours if his hourly pay is $11?

$T = hd$ $\qquad$ $T = 24 \times \$11$ $\qquad$ $T = \$264$

6. Batteries sell for $2.50 a pack. How much will 6 packs cost? How much will 10 packs cost?

7. A field goal in football is worth 3 points. Write a function rule for points scored in a game in terms of the field goals. (Hint: Use variables to stand for total points and number of field goals.)

8. At the video arcade, a regular game costs $1.50 and a video dance game costs $0.25 for 8 minutes. How much do you pay to play one regular game and one video dance game for 48 minutes?

LESSON 19 Tables, Rules, and Graphs

You have learned that equations such as $y = x + 2$ are called linear equations because their graphs are lines. Linear equations are also functions. For each *x*-value, there is exactly one *y*-value.

The table of numbers shows a function with the rule $y = 2x$.

The input values are in the *x*-column. The output values are in the *y*-column.

You can use the table of *x* and *y* values to graph the function on a coordinate plane.

x	y
0	0
1	2
2	4
3	6

Example

In an hour of tennis, you might burn 300 calories. Graph this function. Rule: $y = 300x$.

STEP 1 Make a table of values using input and output.

Time (hours)	1	2	3	4
Calories burned	300	600	900	1,200

STEP 2 Plot the ordered pairs.

(1, 300), (2, 600), (3, 900), and (4, 1,200)

STEP 3 Draw a line through the points.

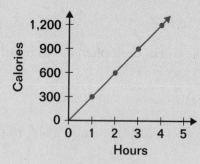

ON YOUR OWN

Whenever they play table tennis, Julia gives Ramona a 3-point head start. Draw the graph of the function $y = 3 + x$.

Practice

Building Skills

Use the information in the function table to graph the function. You can use the coordinate plane on page 80 to help you.

1.

x	y
0	4
1	5
2	6

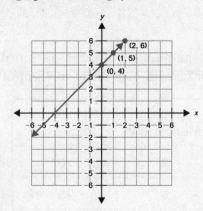

(2, 6)
(1, 5)
(0, 4)

2.

x	y
−1	−3
0	0
1	3

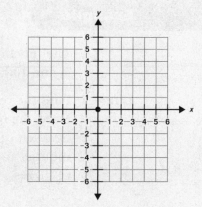

3.

x	y
−1	−3
0	−1
1	1

Use the function rule to graph the function. Label each graph and write its function rule.

4. $y = x - 2$

5. $y = 3x - 1$

6. $y = \dfrac{x}{2}$

7. $y = -2x - 3$

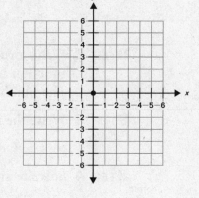

Problem Solving

Find the function rule. Then graph the function on a coordinate plane.

8. Peaches cost $1 more per pound than pears. The price of peaches is a function of the price of pears.

The rule: Let x stand for the price of pears, and let y stand for the price of peaches. Then make a table of x- and y-values.

9. A grocery delivery service charges $3 per delivery.

10. Whatever number Naomi picks, Lin picks one that is 2 more than twice Naomi's number.

TEST-TAKING STRATEGY

Write an Equation

Writing an equation can help you answer test questions about functions.

Example

The function table below shows the number of pizzas Jack ordered in 2, 5, 7, and 10 months. How many pizzas will Jack order in 15 months?

STEP 1 Find the relationship. Here, the relationship is between the number of months and the number of pizzas.

Number of Months (m)	Number of Pizzas (p)	
2	10	← $2 \times 5 = 10$
5	25	← $5 \times 5 = 25$
7	35	← $7 \times 5 = 35$
10	50	←$10 \times 5 = 50$
15	?	

STEP 2 Write a rule for the function in words.
The number of pizzas is 5 times as much as the number of months.

STEP 3 Write the rule as an equation.

$p = 5 \times m$, or $p = 5m$

STEP 4 Solve using the rule and the known values.

$p = 5 \times 15, p = 75$

Jack will order 75 pizzas in 15 months.

TRY IT OUT

Suppose the numbers in the second column of the function table above were 9, 12, 14, and 17. Find the new rule. How many pizzas are now ordered after 15 months?

Circle the correct answer.

A. 30   **B.** 21   **C.** 23   **D.** 22

Option D is correct. The function rule is $p = m + 7$. Therefore, in 15 months he will order $15 + 7$ or 22 pizzas.

Give the function rule and the next 3 terms of each sequence.

1. 4, 11, 18, 25, ... _____

2. 16, 18.5, 21, 23.5, ... _____

3. 800, 400, 200, 100, ... _____

4. 1, −2, 4, −8, ... _____

The table shows prices for viewing sporting events from a cable company. Use the information in the table to solve Problems 5–7.

Sporting Event Viewed	1	2	3
Price in Dollars	5.50	11	16.50

5. You pay $33 to view several sporting events. How many events do you see for that price?

6. What rule can you write for adding amounts to the Price in Dollars row?

7. What function rule can you write for this table of values?

Write a function rule for the input/output relationship between *x*- and *y*-values.

8. _____

x	1	2	3	4
y	6	7	8	9

9. _____

x	1	2	3	4
y	3	5	7	9

Use the function table to graph the function.

10.

x	y
0	3
1	4
2	5

11.

x	y
−1	1
0	3
1	5

Use the function rule to graph the function. Label each graph and its function rule.

12. $y = x - 3$

13. $y = 2x + 1$

Real-Life Matters

You and your younger brother are at an amusement park. In front of one of the rides is a sign that says your height must be greater than or equal to 48 inches. This information can be expressed as an inequality.

$h \geq 48$

h is a variable for height

$\geq$ means *equal to or greater than*

When you measure your brother, you will find out if his height is greater than or equal to 48 inches.

Real-Life Application

You can check your brother's height easily at the park. How could you find his exact height?

_____

_____

If your brother measured exactly 48 inches, could he still get on the ride? Explain.

_____

_____

How could you find how much greater your height is than your brother's? How would you express this fact using symbols?

_____

_____

List some situations when you would need to compare numbers that are not equal in value?

_____

_____

Overview • Lessons 20–21

Writing and Graphing Inequalities

If Edwin travels by plane, his bag cannot weigh more than 60 pounds. Edwin thinks his bag weighs less than 60 pounds. How do you write this information using numbers? How do you show it on a graph?

You know that one amount is equal to another when you hear words like *the same as* or *equal to*:

The price of 4 tickets is equal to $5.

You also know that you can write number sentences instead of word sentences.

How do you write number sentences that mean *up to, less than, more than, at most, greater than or equal to,* or *at least as much as*? These expressions describe unequal amounts.

There are symbols that show amounts that are unequal, just as there are symbols that show amounts that are equal. In the two lessons that follow, you will learn what **inequalities** are and how to write them with symbols and on a graph.

YOU KNOW

- That an equation shows two expressions are equal

- How to write and graph equations

- How to locate integers on a number line

YOU WILL LEARN

- How to write an inequality

- How to graph inequalities on a number line

Remember the BASICS

Solve each equation.

1. $6 + 9 \div 3 = x$

$6 + (9 \div 3) = x$

$6 + 3 = x$

$x = 9$

2. $3x + 15 \div 5 = 23$

3. $\dfrac{4x}{6} \times 4 = 2$

4. $x + 8 \times 3 \div 6 = 3x$

LESSON 20   Inequalities

$h \geq 48$

This statement is an *inequality*. It uses symbols to state that a certain number is *greater than or equal to* 48.

An **inequality** is a number sentence that contains $<$, $>$, $\leq$, or $\geq$.

Symbol	What it means	How it looks on a number line	What the number line shows
$a < b$	a is less than b		a is to the left of b
$a > b$	a is greater than b		a is to the right of b
$a \leq b$	a is less than or equal to b		a is to the left of or equal to b
$a \geq b$	a is greater than or equal to b		a is to the right of or equal to b

You can use inequalities to express real-life situations.

Example

The price of a movie ticket is *more than* $6. Write this information as an inequality.

STEP 1 Pick a variable to stand for the unknown number.
Let p stand for the unknown price of a ticket.
The words *more than* tell you that the price is *greater than* $6. Therefore you will use the $>$ symbol in your inequality.

STEP 2 Write the inequality using the variable.

$p > 6$

ON YOUR OWN

Snacks at the movie theater cost at least $4.

Practice

Building Skills

Write an inequality for each word sentence.

1. 4 is more than y.

> $>$ means is *greater than.* $4 > y$

2. 5 is less than w.

3. $m - 1.5$ is greater than 12.

4. 4.2 is less than m.

5. 0.7 is no greater than r.

6. x divided by 3 is at least as great as 7.

Write a word sentence for each inequality.

7. $4 > b$

> 4 is greater than some number, b.

8. $m \leq -3$

9. $n + 4 \geq 0$

10. $\dfrac{n}{10} > 14$

Problem Solving

Write an inequality to describe each situation.

11. The temperature dropped at least 5 degrees in the last hour.

> Start by choosing a variable to show what the temperature *had been* an hour ago.
> $d \geq -5$

12. The puppy has gained at least 8 pounds since the spring.

13. The mark-up at a clothing store is at least 20%.

14. Prices are above $200.

15. Customers pay no more than $9.95 for anything at the discount store.

16. Including $28 in tips, you will earn at least $100 for your afternoon's work.

LESSON 21   Graphing Inequalities

To go on the ride, you had to be at least 48 inches tall. The inequality $h \geq 48$ shows this situation, but the equation $h = 60$ does not.

Many numbers make the inequality true, but only one number makes the equation true.

When you graph an inequality, you need to show all the possible answers.

Remember the symbols for inequalities are $<$, $>$, $\leq$, and $\geq$. The chart shows how to graph these four kinds of inequalities.

Inequality	How it looks on a graph	What the graph shows
$a < 4$	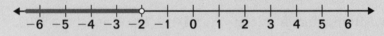	a is less than 4
$a > 4$		a is greater than 4
$a \leq 4$		a is less than or equal to 4
$a \geq 4$		a is greater than or equal to 4

Arrows show that all numbers in that direction are solutions to the inequality.

Example

Graph the inequality $y < -2$.

STEP 1 Understand what the inequality means.
Think: Any number *less than* -2 is a solution. But -2 is not part of the solution because the answer cannot be equal to -2.

STEP 2 Decide which numbers are part of the solution.
Draw a line with an open circle at -2.

ON YOUR OWN

Graph the inequality $y \leq -1$.

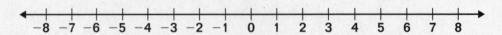

Practice

Building Skills

Graph each inequality.

1. $n > 3$ (number line from −6 to 6 with open circle at 3, shaded to the right)

2. $w \leq 5$

3. $t < -3$

4. $s \leq 0$

5. $x \geq 0$

Write the inequality each graph shows.

6. (number line from −6 to 6, open circle at −1, shaded to the left) _____

7. (number line from −6 to 6, closed circle at 2, shaded to the right) _____

8. (number line from −6 to 6, closed circle at 4, shaded to the left) _____

9. (number line from −6 to 6, open circle at −3, shaded to the right) _____

10. (number line from −6 to 6, closed circle at 0, shaded to the right) _____

Problem Solving

Write an inequality. Then draw a number line and graph the inequality.

11. There are at least 6 new movies that Karen wants to see.

> Start by understanding the inequality.
> *Think:* 6 is part of the solution.
> $x \geq 6$

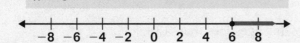

12. If you are at least 12 years old but not yet 17 years old, you can see some, but not all, of the movies at the theater.

Draw a Graph

Drawing a graph will help you answer test questions about inequalities.

Example

Riders need to be at least 4 feet tall to ride a roller coaster. How tall are the riders who could ride the roller coaster?

STEP 1 Write an inequality to describe the situation.
Let h represent the heights of the riders who could ride the roller coaster.

heights of   minimum
the riders (ft)   height (ft)
      ↓   ↓
      h $\geq$ 4

The heights of the riders who could ride the roller coaster are greater than or equal to 4 feet.

STEP 2 Graph the inequality $h \geq 4$.

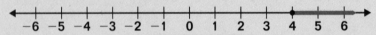

TRY IT OUT

No one younger than 13 can see a film rated PG-13 in the movie theater. What ages *cannot* see a PG-13 film in the movie theater?

Circle the correct answer.

A. $a < 13$ **B.** $a \leq 13$ **C.** $a > 13$ **D.** $a \geq 13$

Option A is correct. The inequality $a < 13$ represents ages less than 13.

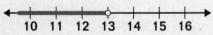

Overview • Lessons 22-23

Solving Inequalities

Hiroko goes into the city to shop. She takes $200. She spends $25 on bus tickets and magazines. She buys a scarf for $40. She is thinking about buying a pair of jeans that cost *at least* $65. If she buys the jeans, how much money will she have left to spend in the bookstore and shoe store?

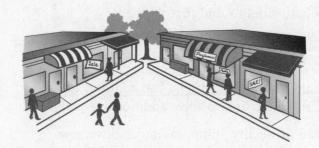

Later, at the bookstore, Hiroko thinks about buying 4 books. Each book costs *between* $10 and $12. If she pays with three $20 bills, how much change will she get back?

These problems are inequalities. They have more than one answer.

To find the answers to these questions, you will need to solve an **inequality**. In the next two lessons, you will learn how to solve inequalities.

YOU KNOW

- How to solve an equation

- How to get the variable on one side by adding or subtracting

- How to get the variable on one side by multiplying or dividing

YOU WILL LEARN

- How to solve inequalities by adding or subtracting

- How to solve inequalities by multiplying or dividing

Remember the BASICS

Solve each equation. If you need to review these skills, turn to page 20.

1. $x + 5 = -12$

   $x + 5 - 5 = -12 - 5$

   $x = -17$

2. $x - 3 = 21$

3. $4x = -24$

4. $2x + 5 = 17$

5. $3x - 3 = -9$

6. $\dfrac{x}{4} + 5 = 10$

LESSON 22

Solving Inequalities by Adding or Subtracting

An equation is solved when the variable is alone on one side of the equation. You solve inequalities in the same way. To solve the equation $n + 3 = 5$, subtract 3 from both sides to find that $n = 2$.

Look at the *inequality* $n + 3 > 5$. If you subtract 3 from both sides, the scale would still be unbalanced.

Addition and subtraction are **inverse** operations. Use addition to solve subtraction inequalities. Use subtraction to solve addition inequalities.

Many solutions can solve an inequality. In the example above, any number greater than 2 is a solution: $3 + 3 > 5, 4 + 3 > 5, 5 + 3 > 5$, and so on.

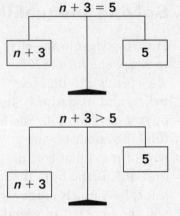

If you add the same number to or subtract the same number from both sides of an inequality, the relationship between the two sides stays the same.

Example

Solve. $n - 4 < 6$

STEP 1 Add or subtract a number to both sides of the inequality so that n is left alone on one side.
Choose a number to add. Then add 4 to undo the subtraction of 4 from n.
$n - 4 + 4 < 6 + 4$

STEP 2 Simplify.
$n < 10$ *All* numbers less than 10 are solutions to $n - 4 < 6$.

STEP 3 Check your answer.
Substitute *any* number less than 10.

Try 9: $n - 4 < 6 \rightarrow 9 - 4 < 6 = 5 < 6$

Therefore, $n < 10$.

ON YOUR OWN

Solve. $y + 2 \leq 7$

Practice

Building Skills

Solve each inequality.

1. $x + 8 < 14$

    $x + 8 - 8 < 14 - 8$
            $x < 6$

2. $y - 5 > 3$

3. $n + 5 \leq 12$

4. $h - 16 > 7$

5. $w + 24.5 < 40.8$

6. $30 + n > 55$

Solve each inequality. **Draw a number line and graph the solution.** *Note:* Remember when to use an open circle and when to use a shaded one.

7. $w + 3 > 6$

8. $m - 8 \leq 2$

9. $24 \leq k + 16$

Problem Solving

Write an inequality to solve each problem.

10. Jack spent less than $15 on a shirt. How much change will he get if pays with a $20 bill?

Let c stand for the amount of change.
$20 - c < 15$

11. Keisha spent 25 minutes fixing her dinner. She thought it would take at least 30 minutes. How much faster did she fix dinner than she thought she could?

12. Cotton T-shirts at the designer store cost at least $5 more than the same shirts at the discount store. The other shirts cost $18. How much would the designer shirts cost?

13. You are allowed to take up to 8 items of clothing into a dressing room. You have taken in at least 5 garments. How many more can you take in?

14. Milton spent $50 on a sweatshirt. Evan spent less than 20% more on the same sweatshirt. How much did Evan spend?

15. A clothing store is having a big sale. Prices are $6 lower for every pair of jeans in the store. The highest price for jeans is regularly $52, and the lowest price is $38. What will the sale prices be?

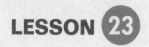

LESSON 23 · Solving Inequalities by Multiplying or Dividing

When you solve equations involving multiplication or division, you multiply or divide both sides by the same number. For example, to solve the equation $8n = 40$, you divide both sides by 8 to find that $n = 5$.

You solve inequalities using multiplication and division in the same way. Multiply or divide each side by the same number. There may be many possible solutions.

- If you multiply or divide both sides of an inequality by a *positive* number, the relationship between the two sides stays the *same*. The inequality sign will face the *same* direction.
- If you multiply or divide both sides of an inequality by a *negative* number, the relationship between the two sides *changes*. The inequality sign will face the *opposite* direction.

Example

Solve. $-4n < 12$

STEP 1 Multiply or divide both sides of the inequality.
Use a number so that n is left alone on one side. In this example, divide by -4.

$-4n \div -4 > 12 \div -4$

Reverse the inequality symbol.

STEP 2 Simplify.
$n > -3$

All numbers greater than -3 are solutions to $-4n < 12$.

STEP 3 Check your answer.
Substitute any number greater than -3.

Try -2: $-4(-2) = 8$

Since $8 < 12$, the answer is true.

Therefore, $n > -3$.

ON YOUR OWN

Solve. $\dfrac{y}{3} \leq 6$

Practice

Building Skills

Solve each inequality.

1. $8x < 24$

$$8x \div 8 < 24 \div 8$$
$$x < 3$$

2. $\dfrac{y}{5} > 3$

3. $-4n \leq 12$

4. $\dfrac{h}{-6} > 7$

5. $6w \leq -48$

6. $3n + 5 > 50$ *Hint:* Undo the addition first.

Solve each inequality. Draw and graph the solution on a number line.
Note: Remember when to use an open circle and when to use a shaded one.

7. $-4w > 20$

8. $\dfrac{m}{2} \leq 3$

9. $24 \geq 8k$

Problem Solving

Write an inequality. Then solve the problem.

10. Jerome spent at least $75 on 3 ties. All three ties were the same price. How much did he spend per tie?

$$\dfrac{x}{3} < 75$$
$$x < 25$$

11. Brita bought 4 bathing suits, each at the same price. She spent less than $120. How much did she pay for each suit?

12. Chin-Sun's parents give her $400 to spend on the 4-day class trip. How much can she spend per day, without spending all her money?

13. According to the sign at the theme park, the swing ride can safely hold 4,500 pounds. If the average child weighs 90 pounds, how many children can safely ride at the same time?

14. Abiola earns $12 per hour. How many hours must she work to earn more than $600?

15. Roberto has saved $100 to buy a mountain bike. If he can save at least $20 a week, how many weeks will it take him to buy a $700 bike?

TEST-TAKING STRATEGY

Write an Inequality

Writing an inequality that includes an operation, such as addition or subtraction, can help you answer some test questions about inequalities.

Example

A private pilot's license requires at least 40 hours of flight time. Kyle flew 5 hours this week, but he has not met the minimum requirement. How many hours does Kyle need to fly?

STEP 1 Write an inequality to describe the situation.
Let n stand for the number of hours Kyle needs to fly.

hours needed		hours logged in this week		hours required
↓		↓		↓
n	$+$	5	$\geq$	40

STEP 2 Solve the inequality.

$n + 5 \geq 40$

$n + 5 - 5 \geq 40 - 5$ — Subtract 5 from both sides of the inequality to get the variable by itself.

$n \geq 35$

Kyle needs at least 35 hours of flight time.

TRY IT OUT

Rachael is tracking the temperature in full sun and in the shade. The temperature in full sun dropped 6°F but is still more than the 70°F temperature in the shade. What is the temperature in full sun?

Circle the correct answer.

A. $t \leq 70°F$ **B.** $t < 70°F$ **C.** $t \geq 76°F$ **D.** $t > 76°F$

Option D is correct. Solve the inequality $t - 6 \geq 70$. $t - 6 + 6 \geq 70 + 6$, so $t \geq 76°F$.

Write an inequality for each sentence.

1. 6 is less than x.

2. 5.5 is greater than y.

Write a sentence for each inequality.

3. $w < 7$ _____

4. $\dfrac{s}{4} + 2 \le 12$ _____

Draw a graph for each inequality.

5. $n > 4$

6. $x \ge 5$

Write the inequality for each graph.

7. _____

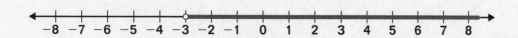

8. _____

Solve.

9. $x + 5 \le 9$

10. $y - 12 < 10$

11. $n + 6.6 \ge 20$

12. $25 + w > 40$

13. $4n < 12$

14. $3y \le 21$

15. $-5x \ge 40$

16. $-3y - 5 > 16$

17. Harold spent less than $12 on a belt. He paid with a $10 bill and a $5 bill. How much change will he get?

18. Kristen earns $11 an hour working at the market. How many hours must she work to earn more than $220?

Post Test

Take this post test after you have completed this book. The post test will help you determine how far you have progressed in building your math skills.

Write an algebraic expression.

1. 6 less than a number _____

2. 2 more than 5 times a number _____

Solve for $x = 2$ and $y = 4$.

3. $3x + 2y$

4. $\dfrac{y}{2}(4 - x) =$

Write an equation.

5. The sum of a number and 1.5 is 7.

6. Nine is 4 more than the quotient of a number and 3.

Solve.

7. $2 + 5 \times 6 =$

8. $3(n + 5) = 39$

9. $y - 4 > 9$

10. $3x \le 15$

11. A carpenter charges $200 per day plus a flat fee of $85 for materials. He works on a job for 3 days. How much does he charge?

12. Pat scored 15 points. Jasmine scored 2 less than double Pat's score. How many points did Jasmine score?

13. When a number y is divided by 4, the quotient is greater than 3. What is the number?

14. Elena saves about $15 a week. How many weeks will it take her to save at least $300?

Give the next 3 terms in each sequence.

15. 2.2, 6.2, 8.2, 12.2 . . . _____

16. 0.03, 0.3, 3, 30 . . . _____

For items 17 and 18 use the coordinate plane below.
Give the coordinates for each point.

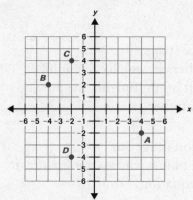

17.   B _____

18.   D _____

19.   Use the table to find the function rule. Then graph the function.

x	y
0	0
1	3
2	6

Find the slope.

20.   (2, 5) and (3, 2) _____

For items 21 and 22 use the coordinate plane below.
Identify the *y*-intercept.

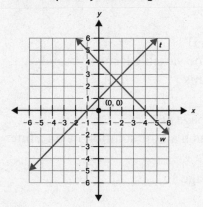

21.   line *t* _____

22.   line *w* _____

23.   Make a table of values. Then graph the
equation $y = 2x + 2$.

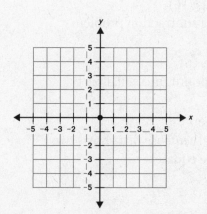

Glossary

addition (page 16)
putting numbers together to find a total

$$
\begin{array}{r}
23 \\
+12 \\
\hline
35
\end{array}
$$

algebraic expression (page 7)
a mathematical expression with at least one variable; $3y - 9$ is an algebraic expression

arithmetic sequence (page 48)
a sequence of numbers in which each number, or term, is the result of adding the previous term by the same number

common difference (page 48)
a fixed number added to a term in an arithmetic sequence to get the next term; in the arithmetic sequence 2, 5, 8, 11, 14... the common difference is 3

common ratio (page 50)
a fixed number multiplied to a term in a geometric sequence to get the next term; in the geometric sequence 2, 10, 50, 250,... the common ratio is 5

coordinate plane (page 34)
a horizontal number line (the x-axis) crossed with a vertical number line (the y-axis)

difference (page 16)
the answer to a subtraction problem

division (page 16)
splitting an amount into equal parts

equation (page 7)
a mathematical *sentence* that shows two expressions are equal

evaluating expressions (page 12)
replacing a variable in an expression with a number

geometric sequence (page 50)
a sequence of numbers in which each number, or term, is the result of multiplying the previous term by the same number

graph of an equation (page 36)
the graph of all the points whose coordinates are the solution to an equation

graph of an inequality (page 66)
a graph that shows all the solutions that satisfy the inequality

horizontal axis (page 34)
the line in a coordinate plane that goes from side-to-side; also known as the x-axis

inequality (page 64)
a mathematical sentence that contains $<, >, \leq, \geq$, or $\neq$

like terms (page 14)
terms with the same variable factors; $2x$, $-3x$, and $4x$ are like terms

linear equation (page 36)
an equation in which all the solution lie on a line

multiplication (page 16)
repeated addition

order of operations (page 10)
work inside parentheses
simplify exponents
multiply and divide from left to right
add and subtract from left to right

ordered pair (page 34)
a set of values for a point on a coordinate plane

origin (page 34)
point $(0, 0)$ on a coordinate plane

point (page 34)
an intersection of the horizontal and vertical values on a coordinate plane

product (page 16)
the answer to a multiplication problem

quotient (page 16)
the answer to a division problem

rise (page 40)
the vertical distance between two points on a line

run (page 40)
the horizontal distance between two points on a line

slope (page 39)
a mathematical representation of how much a line slants upward or downward

$$\text{slope} = \frac{x_2 - x_1}{y_2 - y_1}$$

term (page 14)
a number, variable, or the product or a number and a variable; $3x$, 21, y, and $-2n$ are all terms

variable (page 7)
a letter that stands for an unknown number

vertical axis (page 34)
the line in a coordinate plane that goes from up-and-down; also known as the y-axis

x-axis (page 34)
horizontal number line on coordinate plane

x-coordinate (page 34)
the first number in an ordered pair

y-axis (page 34)
vertical number line on coordinate plane

y-coordinate (page 34)
the second number in an ordered pair

y-intercept (page 39)
the point at which a line intersects the y-axis

Math Toolkit

Coordinate Plane

You can use this blank coordinate plane to help you plot points and graph functions.

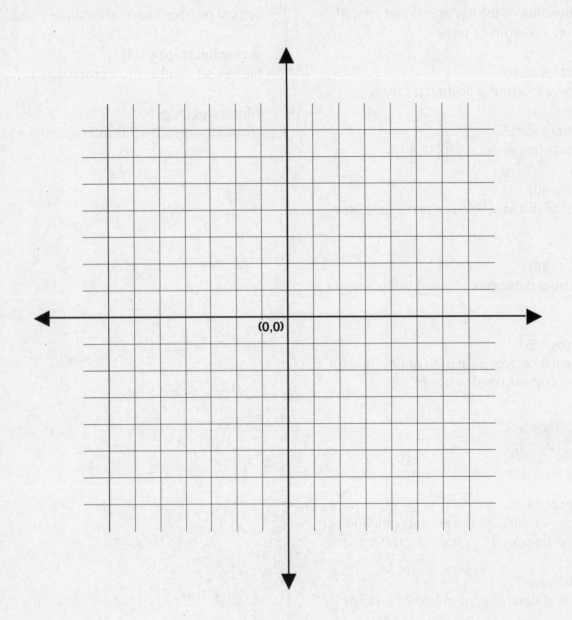

Function Table

A **function table** has input values and output values.

For any input value in a function table, there is only one output value. You can use the table below to help calculate the x- and y-values for a function.

Place the function in the space between the x and y columns. Choose several values for the x-variable. Plug the value for the x-variable into the function and solve for y.

x		y	ordered pairs

Math Toolkit

Creating Equations

An algebraic **expression** is a mathematical *phrase* containing at least one variable.

An algebraic **equation** is an algebraic *sentence* that shows how two expressions are equal.

When you write an algebraic equation use the following steps:

STEP 1 Identify what you know and do not know.

STEP 2 Write a sentence that describes what you know.

STEP 3 Choose a variable to stand for each of the unknown quantities. Usually, your variables are *x* and *y*.

	y-variable	equals	*x*-variable	operation	quantity
Sentence (from STEP 2)		equals			
Equation		=			

STEP 4 Write the equation.

Math Toolkit

Math Symbols

$\overline{AB}$	line segment
=	equals or equal to
≈	approximately equal to
>	greater than
<	less than
~	similar to
°	degrees
∠	angle
△	triangle
π	pi
⊥	perpendicular to
‖	parallel to
√	square root
≅	congruent to
≤	less than or equal to
≥	greater than or equal to

Math Toolkit

To Graph an Inequality

- Locate the number in the inequality on the number line.

- If x is $>$ a number, use an open circle on the number on the number line and shade the number line to the right.

- If $x \geq$ a number, place a closed circle on the number line and shade the number line to the right.

- If x is $<$ a number, place an open circle on the number line and shade the number line to the left.

- If x is $\leq$ a number, place a closed circle on the number line and shade the number line to the left.

Examples:

$x > 4$

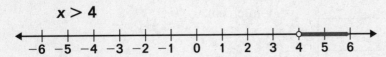

$x \geq 4$

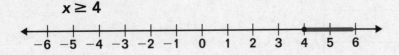

$x < 4$

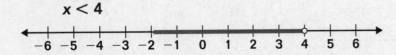

$x \leq 4$

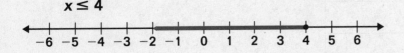

Math Toolkit

Finding Slope Using Slope-Intercept

As you learned in Lesson 13 slope measures the slant of a line from left to right. The **slope** of a line is a ratio of the vertical distance between two points on a line (the **rise**) and the horizontal distance between the two points (the **run**).

You can also determine the slope of a line when an equation is written in **slope-intercept form**. An equation in slope-intercept form is written $y = mx + b$. The equation $y = 5x + 3$ is written in slope-intercept form. The equation $2x - 3y = 10$ is <u>not</u> in slope-intercept form. In slope intercept form m = the slope and b = the y-intercept.

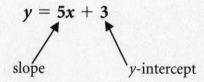

$$y = 5x + 3$$

slope y-intercept

Therefore, in the equation above, the slope = 5 and the y-intercept is at point (0, 3).